# PONY

## THE ANNUAL!

**2009**

# What's in PONY THE ANNUAL!

PAGE 74

PAGE 90

PAGE 86

PAGE 44

**PAGE 78**

**PAGE 60**

**PAGE 68**

**PAGE 26**

**PAGE 64**

WHAT ARE YOU WAITING FOR? TURN THE PAGE AND GET READING!

# Part One

# The A – Z of horses

## A is for...

**Artificial aids** – whips, spurs and any anything else used to help control the pony when you are riding.

**Azoturia** – when the muscles in the back and hindquarters stiffen and spasm. Also called tying-up.

## B is for...

**Bars of the mouth** – the space between a pony's teeth, where the bit lies.

**Barley** – a type of feedstuff that is very high in energy.

**Bitless bridle** – a bridle that has no bit attached. Pressure is applied to the nose, chin and poll, rather than the mouth.

**Blanket clip** – where hair is clipped from the head, neck and belly, but the body and legs are left on for warmth.

**Bot fly** – A nasty little bug that lays its eggs on ponies. When the larvae hatch, they burrow into the skin and travel to the stomach! The eggs are tiny and yellow, and if you see them on your fave pony's coat, tell an experienced person so they can remove them, quick!

**Boxy feet** – Hooves that are very upright instead of slanted.

**Brushing** – when the hoof or inside of the fetlock strikes the inside of the opposite leg.

## C is for...

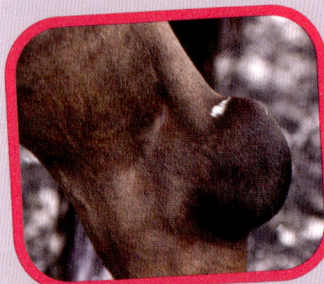

**Cannon bone** – the bone that runs from the knee/hock to the fetlock.

**Capped hocks** – fluid on the hock following an injury or knock.

**Cast** – when a horse gets stuck against the wall of a stable when lying down or rolling.

**Colt** – a male foal up t[o] the age of four.

**Coronet band** – where the pastern meets the hoof.

**Cow-hocked** – a conformation fault where the hocks turn in towards each other making them weak.

**Cavesson** – a basic, flat noseband, or a special type of headcollar used when lungeing.

**Crib-biting and windsucking** – vices where the pony bites onto something and gulps air into the stomach.

## D is for...

**Dishing** – when a pony's foreleg swings outward from the knee in a circular motion, especially in trot.

**Dorsal stripe** – a dark strip running along the spine from the wither to the tail.

## E is for...

**Ergot** – the little horny growth found at the back of the fetlock. It's though[t] to be the remains of when horses had three toes, millions of years ago

**Ewe neck** – a weak neck with no muscle that appears to look concave rather than convex.

## F is for...

**Feather** – the long hair on the lower part of ponies' legs.

**Flehmen** – when a pony curls its top lip to smell or taste the air.

**Flying change** – when the horse changes its canter lead without breaking the canter.

# nd ponies!

**O**ur ultimate pony A – Z guide! We've left out the everyday things and added some more unusual ones! Test yourself on pages 28-29.

## G is for...

**Green** – a young or inexperienced horse.

## H is for...

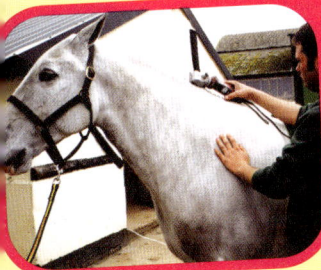

**Hogged mane** – where a pony's whole mane is cut off with clippers.

**Half-halt** – used to re-balance or steady your pony when riding. A firm but gentle check and release action with the outside rein whilst, keeping the leg on.

**Hunter clip** – where the head, neck and body is clipped out, leaving hair only on the legs and a saddle patch area.

## I is for...

**Independent seat** – when a rider has got to a certain level where they are in balance and harmony with the horse's movement, and don't have to rely on the reins or stirrups for balance.

## J is for...

**Jenny** – a female donkey.

**Jump off** – the final round in a showjumping class where riders who jumped a clear round in the first round must ride against the clock to try to get the fastest round and win the class!

## K is for...

**Knee boots** – usually made of leather and used when travelling or riding on the road to protect the pony's knees from knocks or falls.

## L is for...

**Laminitis** – a very painful inflammation in the foot which can be treated if caught early, but can also be very serious if it's left.

**Leg-yield** – a school movement in which the horse moves sideways at the same time as forwards by crossing his legs over.

**Linseed** – a feedstuff that is full of oil which is great for putting on condition and giving a glossy coat. It must be soaked and boiled before being fed.

**Lymphangitis** – inflammation and swelling in the legs, usually after an infection has entered the system through a wound.

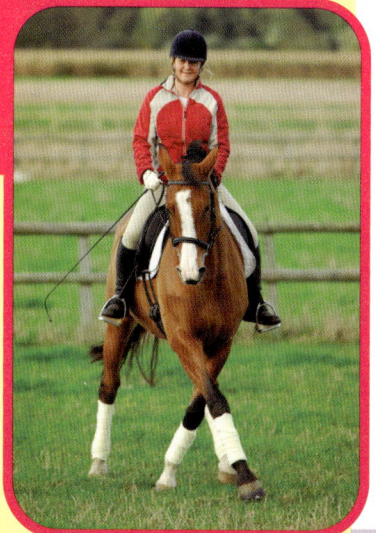

## M is for...

**Martingale** – an artificial aid which stops a pony throwing his head up. Running and standing are the most common types.

**Molasses** – a sugary by-product that can be fed to horses. It's high in energy and very yummy!

**Mud fever** – a condition most common in winter where bacteria in mud gets into the skin of the lower legs and causes red, painful sores. These will scab over but have ooze and puss underneath. It can be very painful if left, but is easy to treat and manage.

Part two is on page 56-57!

9

Whether it's your first time at dressage, or you're a seasoned dressage competitor, here's the PONY guide on how to up the stakes and be a dressage diva!

# Be a dressage

## Before you go...

Know your test. They're all different, so practise on foot (in the garden with markers), or with a model pony on the table indoors. Dressage divas don't practise the whole test on their ponies, just in case their equine partners anticipate the movements and make transitions too early – but you need to be able to do all the movements in the test!

**Stay focused on what you are doing**

## Before you go, two...

Find out when you are due to ride your test – call the organisers if they don't send you your time. This saves hanging about all day!

## When you get there

Tell the organisers you're there and get your number. Then, decide how long you need to warm up. Ride your pony quietly and confidently, and practise a few moves to get him attentive an listening to you. Keep an eye on the time and stay calm!

## In the arena

Breathe out and look up. The more confident you look, the more confident you will feel. If you smile, your body will relax, your pony will feel good, and you'll look super confident to the judge!

Ride just as you do at home – and stay focused on what you're doing. There may be distractions for you and your pony, but try to block them out. The next few minutes is all about you!

## What if it goes wrong?

Missed a movement? Had a terrible transition? Forgotten the way? Don't panic! You'll only lose marks for that movement, so don't throw the rest of your test by giving up. Simply go on to the next movement and take it from there. You can still get a fab mark!

# diva!

Practise a few moves before your test

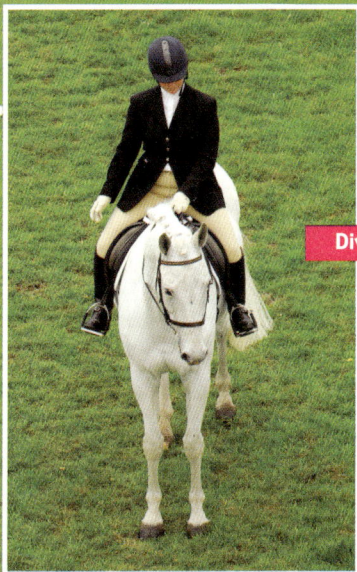

Diva salute!

## Super salute

Make your salute to the judge crisp and unhurried. Practise at home so you look the business!

## When it's all over

Phew! But don't stop riding until you've left the arena. It's not over yet!

## Afterwards

Make sure your pony is comfortable and then have a think about your test. How did it go? It's a good idea to analyse which bits you did well, and which bits you think you need to work on. Then, when you get your test sheet back, you can see whether the judge agrees with you.

## Paperwork

Treat your test sheet like your friend – it will tell you what you need to work on! Read the judge's comments and remember to take notice of the positive things they say, not just the negative things!

## Remember, remember

If you really can't remember your test, you can have someone call it for you, but this can be a bit off-putting. Only you know which you prefer.

## It's you against... you!

Dressage is a sport where you really compete against yourself. It's a great way of measuring how well your schooling is progressing and the idea is to get better marks each time.

# GOOD LUCK IN YOUR DRESSAGE DIVA QUEST!

# CAMPING CAPERS!

Four friends have planned to camp out at the yard in the spare paddock, but will the weather put pay to their plans?

Julie

Sophia

Harriet

Catherine

I'll bring marshmallows to toast on the fire!

I can buy us some food.

I'll bring some torches.

I've got some wood for a camp fire at home.

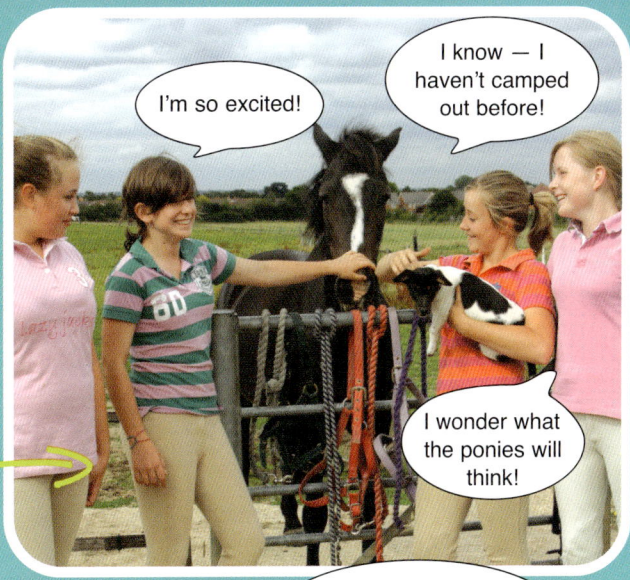

I'm so excited!

I know — I haven't camped out before!

I wonder what the ponies will think!

At least the weather's nice!

Don't speak too soon — there's a big cloud over there...

Let's go for a trot up here!

Okay, we have ages left before it gets dark!

Race you to the top!

Have you seen the tent pegs?

No, have you looked in the tack room?

We've found them! They were in Ben's stable for some reason.

Finally! Can you two come and help put the tent up, then?

Cast: Rhianna as Sophia, Amanda as Julie, Roisin as Harriet and Jessica as Catherine. Issey, Winnie, Nevada and Eddie as themselves!

# CAMPING CAPERS!

Julie

Sophia

Harriet

Catherine

ppee! The tent is up at last!

I can't believe the tent didn't come with an instruction manual!

We'd better get into our pyjamas.

Yum! Toasted marshmallows are the best!

Anyone want to hear my ghost story?

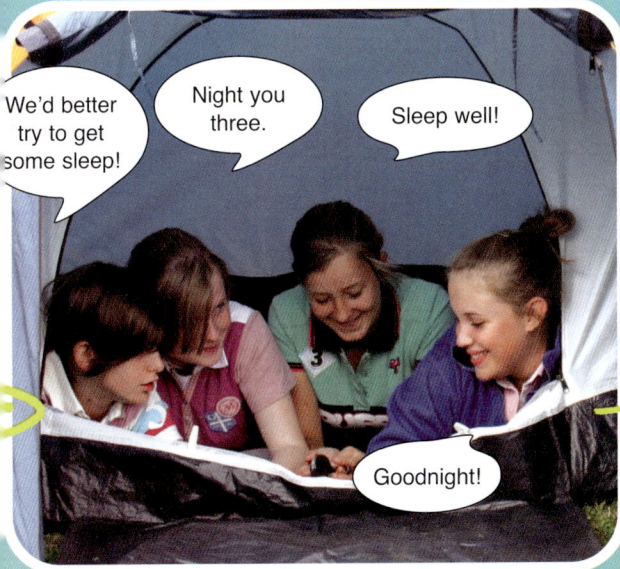

We'd better try to get some sleep!

Night you three.

Sleep well!

Goodnight!

**The following morning...**

I'm shattered. You snored all night Julie!

Yes you did— very loudly!

I did not!

We should do another camp out soon!

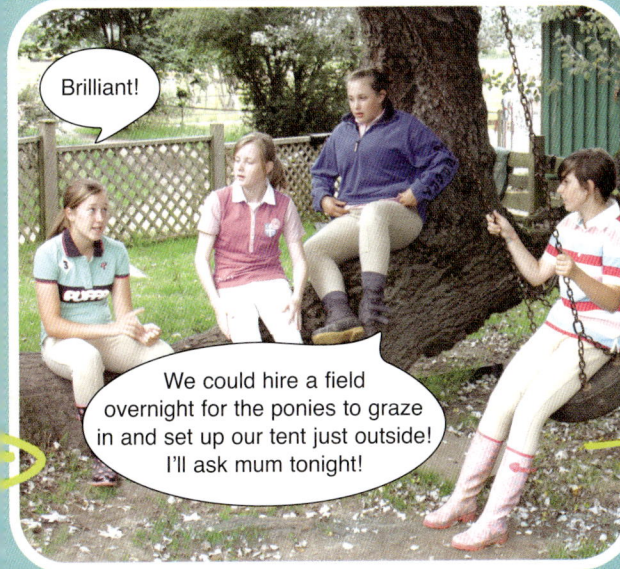

Brilliant!

We could hire a field overnight for the ponies to graze in and set up our tent just outside! I'll ask mum tonight!

Yeah, that was great fun!

And, even better, it didn't rain!

**The end!**

Cast: Rhianna as Sophia, Amanda as Julie, Roisin as Harriet and Jessica as Catherine. Issey, Winnie, Nevada and Eddie as themselves!

# Cracking

## Fact file

Height: up to 12hh

Colour: mainly skewbald, but can also be bay and grey

Characteristics: despite being pony height, the Chincoteague's head is very 'horse-like' in appearance.

## Wild origins

The Chincoteague is one of the last remaining 'wild' horses in the world. They live on the islands of Chincoteague and Assateague, which are found off the coast of Virginia in the USA. There are only about 300 Chincoteague ponies left in the wild today.

It is believed that the Chincoteague breed came about after some ponies were abandoned by colonists back in the 17th century.

## Fowl play

Assateague is also a wild-fowl habitat, protected by the Federal Fish and Wildlife Service of the USA. These birds are often seen standing near to the ponies, and sometimes even sit on the ponies' backs! The ponies don't seem to mind though, as the birds help to reduce the numbers of insects in the area by eating them!

**Chincoteague and Assateague**

16

# Chincoteagues

## Penning days

Every year there are two pony penning days, where all the ponies are rounded up, and the yearlings are auctioned off to raise funds to use towards the management of the herd. In 1933, Assateague became separated from the mainland when there were fierce storms. The ponies have to swim across when they are rounded up, but otherwise they tend to stay on their separate islands.

## Survival of the fittest

The marshlands where the ponies feed also tend to be of poor quality, meaning that only the strongest tend to survive. This has led to the Chincoteague ponies being particularly hardy and adaptable.

## Mini Quiz

1 What year was the book Misty of Chincoteague written?

2 Approximately how many Chincoteague ponies are there left in the wild now?

3 What colour are most of the Chincoteague ponies?

4 In which year did Assateague become separated from the mainland?

5 How many pony penning days are there each year?

**How did you do?** 1) *Misty of Chincoteague* was written in 1947. 2) There are approximately 300 ponies left in the wild. 3) Most of the Chincoteague ponies are skewbald. 4) 1933 is the year when Assateague split from the mainland. 5) There are two pony penning days held each year.

# Make...
# a NAME PLATE
# out of salt dough!

**Salt dough is great fun because you can mould it into any shape you want! Here's a fab way to make a nameplate for either your fave pony's stable, or for your own bedroom door!**

## YOU'LL NEED:

- Flour
- Water
- Salt
- Cooking oil
- Rolling pin
- Baking tray
- Paint in various colours
- PVA glue
- Coloured string

**1** In order to make the salt dough mix 300g of flour, 200ml of water, 300g of salt and 2 tsp of oil together in a bowl. Squeeze it together with your fingers until you can pat it into a ball shape, and then roll it out flat with a rolling pin!

**2** Make a big rectangle shape for the name plate, and then use our template (found on page 99) to make a pony head. You can then roll more dough to spell out your pony's name, or you can paint it on later.

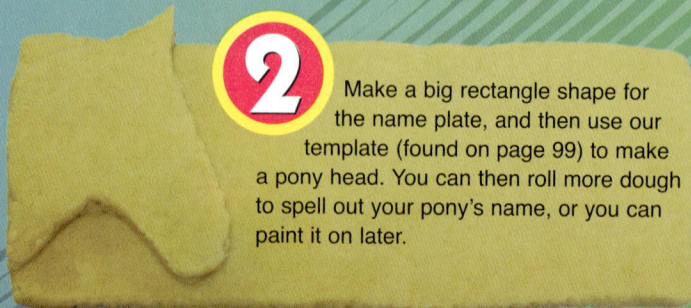

**3** Squash the edges of the pony head and letters onto the nameplate, so that they stick together.

**4** Place on a baking tray and ask an adult to put in the oven for 20 minutes, on Gas mark 4 (180°C).

**5** Leave to cool, and then paint in your fave colours! Make sure that you paint the background first, and allow it time to dry to avoid getting splodges.

**6** Place two paperclips on the back of the nameplate so that they slightly overhang the top. Then cover with PVA glue and leave to dry overnight. Once this layer of glue is dry, carefully see if the paper clips are secure. If not, add another layer of PVA glue.

**7** Tie some string onto each paperclip and hang up your wonderful nameplate! It will look great on your bedroom door, or on your fave pony's stable, but make sure he can't eat it!

# Why do we...?

There's a right way and a wrong way for most of the things we do with horses and ponies – and good reasons for doing them the right way! See if you know the right answers to the *Why do we...?* questions below!

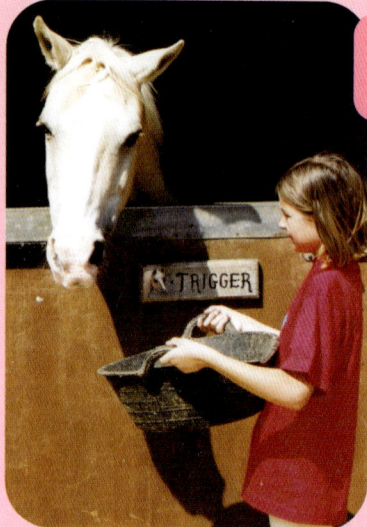

**1** ...rest horses and ponies for an hour after their feed, before we exercise them?

A To let their food digest properly ■
B Because they are waiting for their pudding ■
C So they can pass droppings before exercise ■

**2** ...warm up slowly before doing any fast work?

A Because they don't have a rug on ■
B Because ponies don't like the cold ■
C To stretch the muscles gently ■

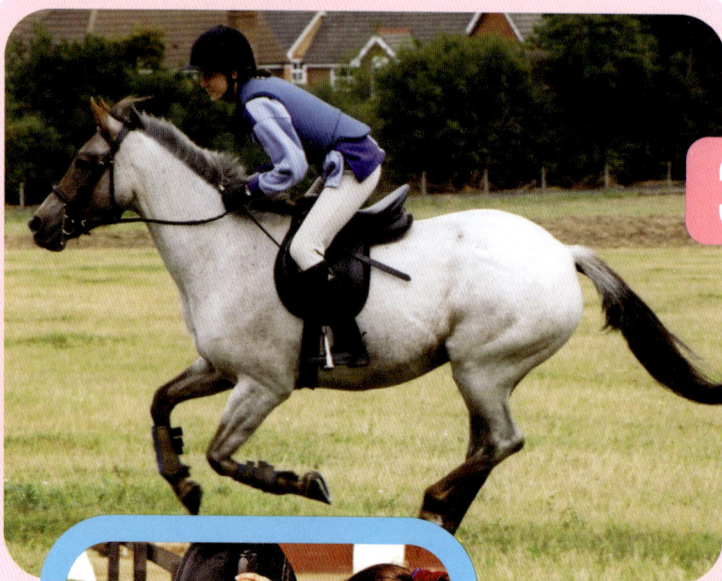

**3** ...avoid cantering or galloping on very hard ground?

A To avoid injury to the legs ■
B To avoid denting the ground ■
C You might squash a flower ■

**4** ...clean tack regularly?

A To show off to your mates ■
B To keep the tack supple and in good condition ■
C Because your pony can see if it's dirty ■

**5** ...pick out horses' feet from frog to toe?

A To stop the hoof from croaking ■
B You don't need to pick out the hooves at all ■
c To avoid injury to the frog ■

**6**

**...tack up, put rugs on, lead horses etc, etc on the left hand side?**

**A** All horses are left handed ■
**B** So that horses get used to being approached on one side ■
**C** Don't take any notice – you can approach from either side ■

**7**

**...not brush a wet, muddy horse?**

**A** It will ruin the brush ■
**B** It will make the horse's hair go spikey ■
**C** It's harmful to brush mud and moisture into the skin ■

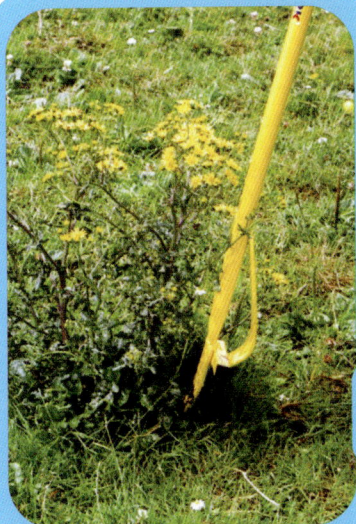

**8**

**...have three girth straps on a saddle but only use two?**

**A** The third is a spare in case another one breaks ■
**B** Three's a lucky number ■
**C** To stop the saddle from slipping ■

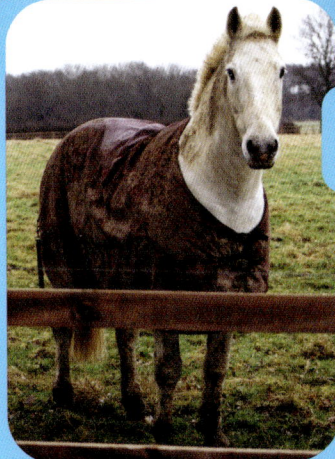

**9**

**...use a quick release knot to tie up?**

**A** To enable the horse to run off easily ■
**B** To enable you to untie quickly in an emergency ■
**C** Because it looks neat ■

**10**

**...dig up and burn ragwort?**

**A** To stop your pony eating this poisonous plant, and to stop it spreading ■
**B** Because it is a funny colour ■
**C** Because the flowers look gorgeous in a vase ■

**More over the page!**

# Why do we...?

**11** **...groom regularly?**

**A** Because you have nothing better to do ■
**B** To keep your pony squeaky clean and in good condition ■
**C** Because it is good exercise for you, and you need to tone up those muscles ■

**12** **...poo-pick fields?**

**A** To remove worms from the field ■
**B** To stop ponies rolling in their poo ■
**C** To make the fields look neat and pretty ■

**13**

**...not let ponies eat too much rich grass?**

**A** It makes them go green ■
**B** It gets caught in their teeth and stuck in their throat ■
**C** Too much can cause laminitis ■

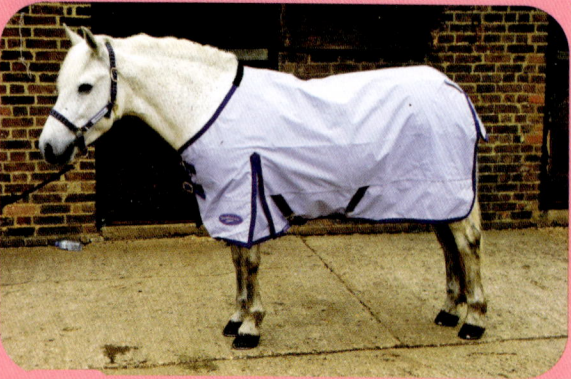

**14** **...put rugs on a little forward and then ease them back?**

**A** So that the pony's coat lies flat ■
**B** Because ponies like the feeling of this ■
**C** To make it easier to do up the rug ■

**15**

**...have a heel on riding/jodhpur boots?**

**A** Because it is *soooo* stylish ■
**B** To stop your foot slipping through the stirrup ■
**C** You don't actually need to have a heel ■

22

**1 A** It takes time for the food to pass through the digestive system, and ponies get colic if they exercise too soon after being fed. So it is really important that you don't feed and then go straight out for a ride – your pony could end up in trouble. It's a bit like us not swimming straight after eating a meal.

**2 c** Horses (and humans!) should always stretch their muscles gently and slowly before starting exercise. That way, the muscles will warm up a little, which makes them less prone to injury. Also, muscles work better when warmed up, so the pony's movement and action will benefit from this.

**3 a** Hard ground has no 'give' – it can be a bit like riding on a hard surface such as a tarmac road. You wouldn't canter or gallop on a road, as you know that this would cause concussion which could injure the delicate structure of the legs. So stick to walk and trot if the ground gets really hard.

**4 b** Leather is a wonderful material in lots of ways, but it needs constant care to keep it supple. If you don't bother to clean and 'feed' it regularly with a good product, then you start to see it getting brittle and, eventually, cracking. And that doesn't just look bad – it can be dangerous as it may break. Not exactly what you want when you are out on a hack!

**5 c** The frog is a sensitive part of the foot, and can be injured (which is why it's important to remove stones from this area). By picking out the hoof going away from the frog (and towards the toe) you make it less likely that you will jab the frog with the hoofpick as you are cleaning the hoof.

**6 b** There's nothing to stop you from doing things from the right-hand side, but it's thought that horses and ponies benefit from us doing things on one side – by convention, this has become the left, probably because most people are right handed. Ponies are creatures of habit, and, it helps that they know we will always be approaching them on the left. You are probably not even aware that you are doing it, as it simply becomes a habit.

**7 c** Brushing wet mud is not good for the skin as it will be brushed into the skin, rather than being brushed off the coat. So, be patient and wait till the mud has dried before getting that dandy brush out! Dry mud comes out so much more easily anyway!

**8 a** Girths are pretty important things, as they keep the saddle on! So it makes sense to have a third girth strap… just in case! When you do up the girth, either use the first and second girth straps, or the first and third, for maximum security.

**9 b** In an emergency, you need to untie the horse or pony you are looking after quickly. If you don't, their natural reaction will be to get away from whatever is frightening them at all costs, which could injure them. A quick release knot is quick and easy to do up in the first place, and is an important knot to use whenever you tie up a pony.

**10 a** Ragwort is a very poisonous plant which, if eaten by horses and ponies, will make them ill, and possibly cause death. So you must remove it from fields, and the best way to do this is to dig it up. This will stop the plant from spreading further (it spreads like wildfire!) and do make sure, when you dig it, that you get the roots out. Leaving just a little bit of root will mean that another plant re-grows in the same spot. Remember to use gloves to protect your hands when handling ragwort, as the toxins in the plant can pass through your skin into your bloodstream, which you don't want either! Ragwort should always be burnt so that there is no chance of it surviving.

**11 b** Regularly grooming has lots of benefits for ponies, the main one being to remove the dirt and keep their coat in good condition. It also gives you the chance to spot any lumps or bumps. You'll find that pampering and grooming is a wonderful bonding time for you both. But take care not to over-groom outdoor-kept ponies, as they need a bit of grease in their coats for protection from the elements.

**12 a** You know how damaging worms are to ponies, in the worst cases causing severe colic and death. The lifecycle starts by ponies eating the worms on a bit of grass, so the best way to stop this happening is to regularly poo-pick the field.

**13 c** Grass is the natural food for horses and ponies – and they love it! In fact, some of them love it too much, and there are some ponies in particular that are prone to that horrible illness laminitis, one of the causes of which is eating too much grass. It is more of a concern in the spring and early autumn, so do take care if you think your pony is at risk. Reduce the amount of time he spends eating the grass, and, although he won't thank you for that, he will thank you for preventing him from getting laminitis which is incredibly painful.

**14 a** If you put a rug on a little forward, and then gently ease it back towards the tail, you will ensure that the hairs on the coat lie flat in the way they normally do. Comfy!

**15 b** It wouldn't be safe if your foot slipped too far through the stirrup, so a proper jodhpur or riding boot heel is essential to prevent this from happening. If you fell off, and your foot was still in the stirrup, you could be dragged. Ouch!

23

# Wild ponies

By Immy Agnew

## A family walking holiday in Wales wasn't Jenny's idea of fun. But then she saw something that changed her mind...

Jenny sighed angrily as the car pulled out of their driveway. The whole family was off to Wales for a walking holiday. Jenny had begged for them to go pony trekking, but had been overruled. Her mum, dad and two brothers had all decided that walking up mountains in deepest, darkest Wales would be great. Jenny was sure it wouldn't be.

"Look on the bright side! If you're lucky, you may see some wild ponies!" her mother had said cheerily. Jenny hadn't replied. She had looked up where they were going on the Internet, and had been told by too many websites that wild ponies weren't seen in that part of Wales.

When they arrived at the old-fashioned cottage, the sky was grey and overcast. It was raining, and even her brother looked doubtful about their choice of holiday. But Jenny secretly rather liked her room. It was small and had a low ceiling, with wooden beams and flowery wallpaper. But the best part was the view from the window; acres and acres of vast countryside – sheep were grazing peacefully and buzzards soared high in the air.

**She saw him, standing on the ridge above the others, proud and majestic: the beautiful black stallion she had seen from her window.**

Jenny decided she was going to make the most of this holiday, even if there were no ponies. She turned to go down to supper, and a startling black movement caught her eye. She turned back to the window, her heart beating. Had she seen a wild pony? Jenny saw a tangle of a wind-whipped tail, heard a loud whinny and then the pony disappeared. She smiled. There *were* wild ponies!

That night, Jenny dreamed she was galloping bareback around the moors on a brilliant black pony. The moon was full and bright, her flimsy nightdress billowed out behind her, but she didn't feel in the least bit cold.

The next day, fat flakes of snow were falling rapidly. Although the rest of the family was downhearted. Jenny felt light and exhilarated. She had a feeling that something special was going to happen. After lunch, she asked if she could go for a walk. The snow had stopped and her parents agreed. Jenny bounced out of the door, slamming it shut behind her, and slid down the path and out of the small garden.

The country air was sharp yet refreshing, and she was soon far from the cottage. Jenny walked briskly for a while, then realised it was time for her to be heading back. She stood proudly on top of a hill, surveying the wide expanse of land. When she couldn't see the cottage, Jenny panicked; she whipped round and looked at the other side of the hill and saw it, miles and miles away, nestled in the depth of the hills. Without her realising, a tear rolled down Jenny's cold cheek. She would never be back before dark.

The snow that had stopped for a while started again with, if anything, more ferocity than before. Jenny ran blindly down the hill, stumbling over rocks hidden by the snow, then tripped on a tree stump and fell forward into the soft, white snow.

Jenny woke suddenly. Where was she? She had fallen... but into the snow. Jenny now found herself amidst lush and green country and there were... ponies! Lots of them! She stood up and a few raised their handsome heads in greeting. There were all colours: chestnut, bay grey, palomino... Jenny suddenly looked around, seeking one pony in particular. She saw him, standing on the ridge above the others, proud and majestic: the beautiful black stallion she had seen from her window.

Jenny ran over to him, light-footed and airy, as if the uneven ground wasn't there. The stallion seemed to have been expecting her and whickered softly. She understood what he wanted, although she didn't know how.

**Jenny laughed out loud. she was galloping at the front of a herd of wild ponies, leading them somewhere special. she could feel their heat, hear the pounding of hooves in her ears, smell the sweet scent of horses.**

Springing onto his broad, shiny back, Jenny sat there with ease. She felt like she could have ridden a racehorse with no danger of her falling off. With a snort and a playful buck, the stallion plunged forward and the herd followed.

Jenny laughed out loud. She was galloping at the front of a herd of wild ponies, leading them somewhere special. She could feel their heat, hear the pounding of hooves in her ears, smell the sweet scent of horses. It was the most fantastic feeling, *ever*!

They slowed to a canter, then to a walk and then stopped. Jenny looked around, puzzled. The pony had brought them outside a large house and it was dark. A young boy tumbled out of the door in his pyjamas, and quickly mounted a slim palomino.

Jenny wasn't the only one with the herd now, but she didn't mind. They stopped at other places until every pony carried a laughing child, and horses and humans were in harmony. They were now riding along a beach, waves crashing against chalky cliffs, the ponies' hooves making prints in the sand.

Suddenly, everything changed; the other children and their steeds disappeared and it was only Jenny and the stallion. They were now cantering through snow, and night was only just beginning to fall. Slowing to a walk, Jenny recognised the little cottage her family was renting. The pony stopped and she slipped off. He stood for a moment, breathing gently on her face.

"Thank you," she whispered. Then he was gone in a flurry of snow.

She stood and watched for a moment, then turned into the house. The magic of the evening was gone. She was just Jenny, who was learning to ride. And he was just a wild stallion who had been abandoned on the Welsh moors.

## Start with a sketch

Horses are a lovely round shape. Include flowing lines and circles in your first sketches to get a pony shape which is not flat on the page. Then fill in the detail, rubbing out your lines and circles as you go.

### Manes and tails

White manes will look empty and lifeless without colour, so add a fe shadow lines with light blue pen.

Black manes ar easiest done with leaving a highlight before. Paint over in dark blue with a light blue highlight.

**Relaxed**

**Attentive**

### Paint job

Once you have your outline, paint the whole body a uniform, light colour. Be careful not to press the pencil too hard on the paper.

### Into the shadows

To make the body look round and real, use shadows for the darker and lighter areas, pressing the pencil harder against the paper.

Remember that areas in the dark need dark shadows, and areas in the light, like the middle of the legs, have a highlight – a lighter shade. Look at the way this horse takes shape and comes to life with shadows and highlights.

# draw!

Here's some expert art tips from PONY illustrators Rebecca Enström and Helena Öhmark, the remarkable talent behind PONY's wonderful Charlie and Jorja illustrations!

**3**

**4**

**7**

## Hooves, who?

When painting black hooves, leave a vertical highlight on the hoof quite near the toe, to make it look round.

If you've made white markings on the legs, the horn of the hoof will be pale or pinkish. To paint pink hooves use a light pink for the whole hoof, leaving a highlight similar to the black ones. To make them look realistic, add a shadow of beige at the edges.

## Eye, eye

Always remember to leave a spot of highlight in the eye to bring it to life.

**Angry or scared**

**Alert**

## It's in the details

To enhance the shape of the body further, apply shadows with a black pencil to:

- the inside of the nostrils
- the underside of the neck
- just under the jaw line
- on the body behind the elbow
- in front of the stifle
- on the upper part of the legs on the off side of the body.

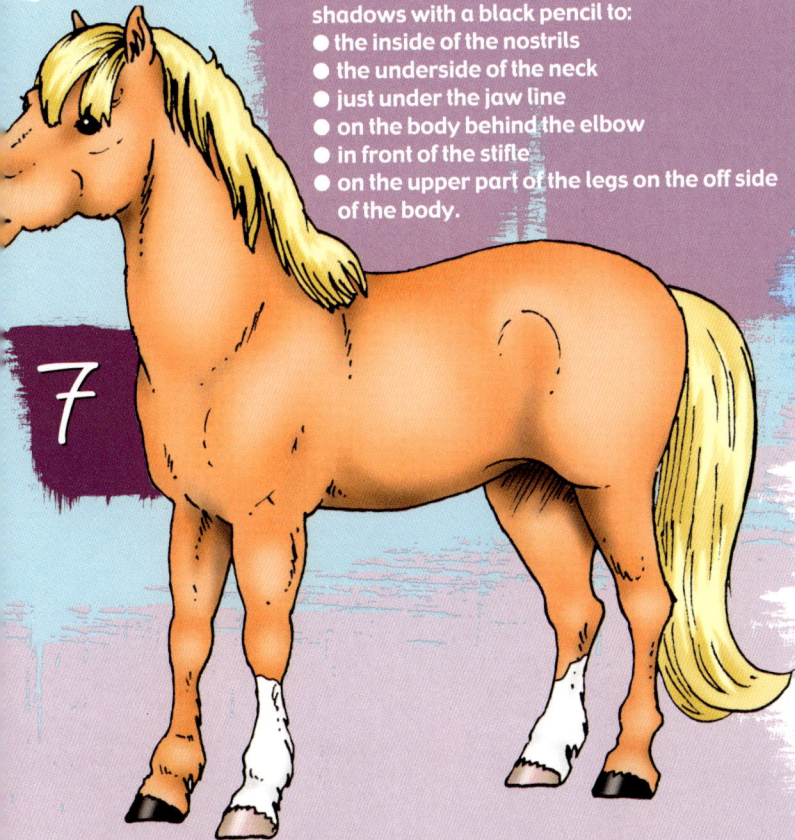

## Pony models

Try drawing and painting ponies using real ones as models. Sit outside a field and sketch away, experimenting with different poses and expressions. And once you're an equine artist extrordinnaire, send Team PONY a piccie!

## Paint job

Be careful not to press too hard with the pencil when applying a black shadow as the nicest effect is achieved with a soft outline rather than a sharp, ink-black shadow. It's far easier to apply more colour than to remove it!

## White horses

White horses, or white markings on the forehead or legs, are easiest done by shadowing lightly with a black pencil around the edges, just like with any other colour. Remember that the highlights will be white instead of lightly coloured.

As with the body, use a light colour and paint the edges darker. Use the pencil in the line of the hair and leave a highlight in the middle or in spots on the tail.

*The small heads show different expressions to inspire you!*

27

# PUZZLE FUN!

## Wordsearch?

**Can you find all these pony colours in our giant wordsearch?**

| | |
|---|---|
| Chestnut | Palomino |
| Piebald | Black |
| Skewbald | Bay |
| Dun | Appaloosa |
| Grey | Brown |
| Cremello | Roan |

```
f p s y r i t s k s r e a n s e
h c h e s t n u t e a h s m e r
i k v r i m l b n e s i o y a v
e r n g a c r e m e l l o j t n
l p o f w r r s t t l m l n q m
w o i m e l f u o i c n a d b h
i i d e b i k s p e p o p s l w
z i d w b a c k d x s t p p i e
c s l c r a a i h s g e a t d i
f c e w o t l r s z y l d x l u
s a l e w l b d a c o a c b a y
g i t d n e m a r m g n a s b t
c v g u b s u p i a l d n m w r
r o a n n t l n o n p t t a e s
e p r p r b o o n e a t l m k r
a c t j l a c g y e n f e y s t
```

## Dynamic duos!

**Can you match these famous riders with the horse they ride? Draw a line to match them up!**

| | |
|---|---|
| Ellen Whitaker | Shaabrak |
| Zara Phillips | Ensign |
| Ben Maher | Omeli |
| Pippa Funnel | Toytown |
| William Fox-Pitt | Lorcano |
| Mary King | Arielle |
| Tim Gredley | Rolette |
| Ollie Townend | Ballincoola |
| Lucy Wiegersma | Flint Curtis |
| William Whitaker | Call Again Cavalier |

# Spot the difference!

**Can you spot the eight difference between these two pictures?**

# Crazy questions!

Have you read our huge pony A-Z on pages 8-9 and 56-57? It's packed full of info! Test how much you've remembered with these teaser questions!

1) What is brushing?_____

2) What is a dorsal stripe?_____

3) When might you use knee boots?_____

4) What is Linseed good for?_____

5) What is ragwort?_____

6) When might you use studs?_____

# Picture crossword

**Can you complete this crossword with just pictures as clues?**

## Across

## Down

29

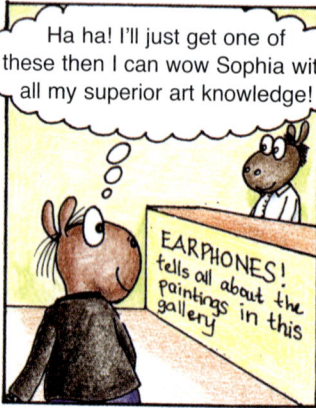

# My BIG mistake!

Olivia's mum, Grace, was one-in-a-million, helping with her pony and supporting her at shows. But was it all too much of a good thing for Olivia, especially when her mum surprised everyone with her new-found skill?

## AS PROUD AS PUNCH!

My mum is my biggest pony supporter and I'm so lucky to have her! She loved coming to watch me compete my pony, Treasure, and better still, she loved helping me get him ready for shows at weekends. She'd give him a bath if he was dirty – which he invariably was, because he's grey and rolls a lot – she'd help clean my tack and she loved grooming.

But as much as she enjoyed being around the yard, she had never ridden – ever! I'd kept going on and on at her to start riding, but she said she just loved helping on the ground. So imagine my surprise when she proudly announced that she'd been having riding lessons on the quiet, and that her instructor at the riding school thought she was capable of going out on a hack. Talk about being surprised... I was gob-smacked! But then, that's Mum for you – full of little surprises!

## OUT AND ABOUT

I keep Treasure at DIY livery on a friend's yard and when they heard that Mum had been having lessons, they said she could borrow one of their horses, so that we could go out on a hack together. Mum wasn't too sure about the idea, as Treasure can get a bit excited out on hacks. However, when I told Mum that we'd just walk and trot, she seemed happy with that and I managed to encourage her to go with me – and we had a great time together.

> I was gob-smacked – but then my mum is always full of little surprises!

In fact, Mum enjoyed her hack so much that we made it a regular thing, and it wasn't long before we were going up a gear and cantering alongside each other – and in control! Mum loved her riding and couldn't get enough of it – she still kept going for her lessons and was soon learning to jump. She seemed to be a natural, and had great balance and a good seat – she was truly bitten by the riding bug.

It wasn't long before Mum was entering little local shows, doing unaffiliated showjumping and dressage competitions on her friend's horse, Tigger. Not only that, but most of the time, she was getting placed, and I will never forget the look of sheer joy on her face when she won her first rosette! Now, however, she's doing better than me and while I know I should be thrilled for her, I'm starting to feel a bit envious of her success.

## CRAMPING MY STYLE!

Most of my friends said how lucky I was to have a mum who is so involved, but I wasn't so sure, as she started to steal my thunder! She began by coming to the stables every spare minute of the day to check up on Treasure and me, and while

everyone at the yard loved her, I never got any time alone with my riding friends. Mum was always there, nagging me to do this right and do that properly! She was starting to cramp my style – I rued the day I ever encouraged her to ride!

Having said that, I was pleased that she was enjoying it and doing well. She didn't really have any hobbies before and always seemed at a loss as to what to do with her day, once she'd decided to give up work in an office. Now, however, she's helping out four days a week at the livery yard and doing most of her riding then, which means that our paths don't cross when I'm down there with my riding friends at the weekends. It also means that Mum now has her own circle of horsey friends during the week, so everyone's happy!

It's great to have a mum who shares my hobby – but I'm glad there's a bit of distance between us now. You can have too much of a good thing!

> I know I should be thrilled for her, but I'm starting to feel envious of her success

posed by models

31

If you want to feel safe and secure in the saddle, then you need a great position – simple, right? Here are a few basic guidelines to help you on your way to developing a great seat!

# perfect posture!

## At Halt

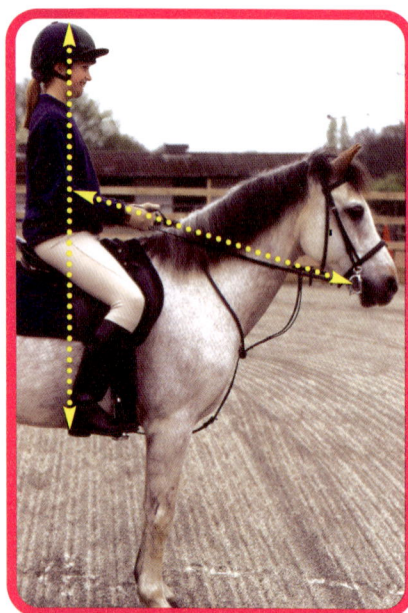

Before you move off, ask yourself the following questions – tick the boxes when you can truthfully answer yes!

**1** Is your seat in the middle of the saddle, your back upright and relaxed and your shoulders back? Can you feel both seatbones in the saddle? Your ears, shoulders, hips and heels should all be in line, as in our picture here. ❏

**2** Are your elbows bent and close to your sides – a straight line from your elbow to your pony's bit, as in our pic? ❏

**3** Are you looking forward, towards where you plan to go? ❏

**4** Are your lower legs maintaining a light contact along your pony's body, slightly behind the girth? ❏

**5** Are your knees softly bent, with light contact between your knees and the saddle? ❏

**6** Are the balls of your feet (the widest part) resting in the stirrups, with your heel lower than your toe? ❏

If the answer is YES to each of these questions, you can go! Try to keep these key points in your mind as you ride, and remember to follow your pony's head movement with your hands as you get going!

## At trot

Maintain that good seat and leg position while trotting. If you are rising to the trot, don't lift yourself out of the saddle too far. The closer you are to the saddle, the less distance you have to sink back, so you'll use less effort, which is more comfy for both you and your pony. Always remember to sit softly in the saddle when you come back down.

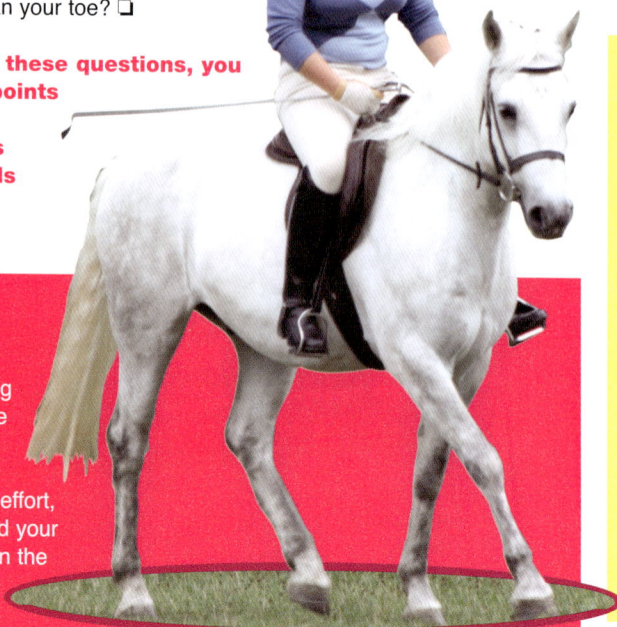

## At canter

Perfecting your seat at canter takes time, and you'll find that it varies from pony to pony – some have an easier movement to sit to! Work on maintaining your lovely upright position, and follow the movement with your hips and seat.

It's important to stay relaxed if you can – if your legs tense up, this might push your bum a little out of the saddle, which is not what you want. Your hands should follow the pony's movement all the time.

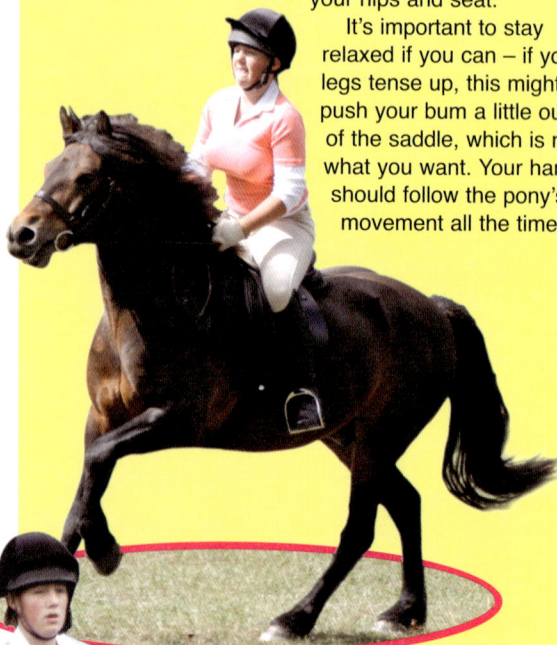

## At gallop

All you have to do here is take a more   position with your upper body, which frees the pony's back for this fast gait. The mistake most people make is letting their lower leg slip back – so if there is one thing you need to remember, it's to keep your strong lower leg position. It will give you security – important when galloping! Again, follow through with your hands, and remember to look up and ahead.

# JUMPING

## THE APPROACH

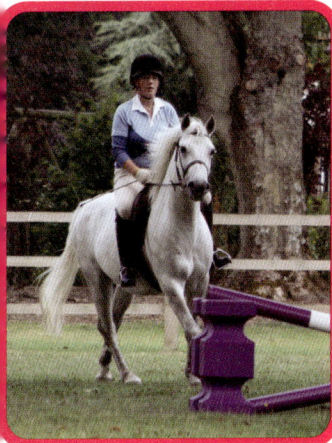

Stay upright with your legs in a good, strong position, looking toward the centre of the jump. Duggie and Charlotte (our models in these three pix) both look alert and ready. There is no need for Charlotte to fold forward at this stage.

## THE JUMP

**Look how strong Charlotte's lower leg position is in this pic!** It's easy for the lower leg to slip back when you fold your upper body forward, but Charlotte has kept her leg where it should be, staying safe in the saddle. She has folded forward a little and her hands have moved up Duggie's neck to let him stretch out and really jump! But she has kept the contact. The pair are working in harmony, which is what riding is all about!

## THE LANDING

Charlotte is returning to her upright position. Her lower legs still look secure and her contact with the reins is good. She's looking toward the next jump.

# DON'T DO THIS AT HOME...!

These elbows need to be nearer their rider's sides.

**This position would be OK for a couch-potato, but needs to be more upright for riding.**

Make sure your shoulders are both at the same height – not uneven like these ones.

**This rider's legs are too far back, so she could easily tip foward if her pony moved off quickly.**

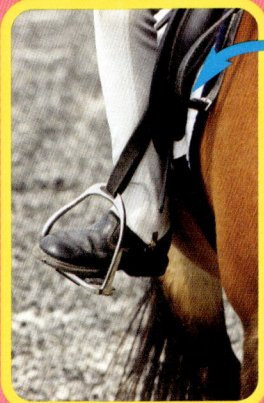

Toes should point forward, not outward!

**Unless you plan to lie back and have a quick nap, it's best not to let your legs come this far forward!**

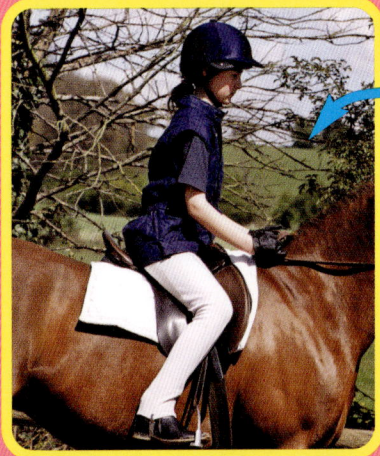

Don't let your upper body tip forward like this – it's not a secure position. Go back and look at the very first *At Halt* pic, with the lines from ear to heel, elbow to bit, to remind you to aim for position perfection at all times!

# Horsey

So you love ponies, right? Of course you do! But how much do you actually understand them? Take our mini quiz to find out!

**A**lthough horses and ponies can't speak, they do have other means of communication, the ears being one of them. Can yu match a pony's ear position to his mood?

**1** You go to catch your fave pony from the field and he is standing with his ears loped to the side. Is he...

a... happy and pleased to see you?
b... dozing and probably hasn't seen you?
c... concentrating hard?

**2** You are riding your fave pony and his ears are out sideways, flicking back and forward every now and then. Is he...

a... unhappy?
b... concentrating and listening to you?
c... about to stop?

**3** Your fave pony puts his ears flat back on his head and pulls a face at another pony. Is he...

a... pleased to see the other pony?
b... scared of the other pony?
c... being threatening or aggressive towards the other pony?

**4** You are out hacking and your fave pony lifts his head high, pricking his ears forward. Is he...

a... interested and looking at something in the distance?
b... bored by his surroundings?
c... a bit grumpy about being ridden?

*ANSWERS!*
1 = b, 2 = b, 3 = c, 4 = a

How did you get on?
Did you get them all right?
Read on and we'll explain all!

### Anxious or scared

When a pony is anxious about something, his ears will be flicked back but not flat against his head. Ponies usually lift or lower their heads to give them a better look at whatever they are worried about.

### Listening or concentrating

The best example of this is when ponies are being ridden. If they are concentrating on what we are asking them to do, the ears will be to the side, constantly flicking back and forward. In this picture, the rider has given an aid with her inside (left) leg. The pony has responded by flicking his left ear back and listening to the aid given.

## Interested or inquisitive

When a pony is being inquisitive and looking at something, he will lift his head and prick his ears forward. If he is listening to something in the distance, the ears will flick toward the sound to try to pick it up.

## Grumpy

When a pony is being grumpy, the ears will go back, but not flat against the head. They will usually pull a bit of a face, too, by screwing up their muzzle – a bit like a grumpy child!

## Bored

Ponies that are bored or sleepy will let their ears lop to the sides. They'll usually drop their head and let their eyes half close, too.

## Happy

When a horse or pony is happy and content his face will look relaxed and the ears will be forwards but not pricked. If your fave pony looks at you like this when he sees you, then you know that he likes you!

## Angry or aggressive

Horses don't generally act aggressively unless they feel threatened. You can tell when a horse is being aggressive as he will pin his ears back flat on his head. Part of the reason for this is so that the funnel-shaped opening is flat against the head, signifying that they cannot hear. "I'm not listening to what you have to say!"

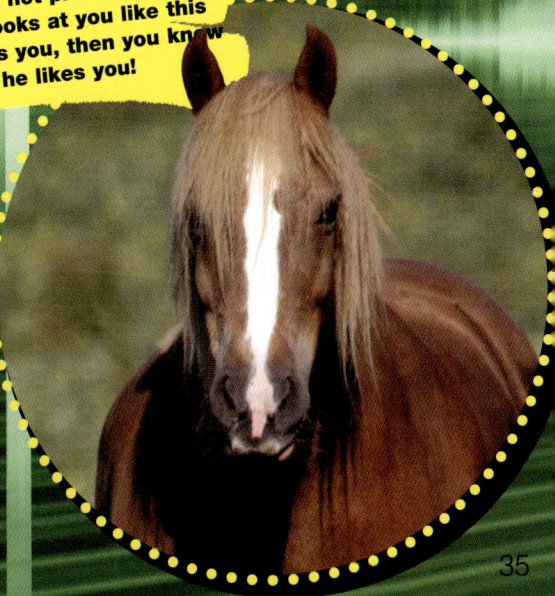

# One in a Million

PONY **Magazine**
short story
competition finalist

## By PONY reader Holly Metcalf

"Well done everyone," Anna, the Pony Club instructor, addressed her 12 pupils, lined up in front of her on their ponies. "That was a great lesson. Your jumping, in particular, has improved a lot."

Megan grinned happily and reached down to pat her pony, Smudge. This was her first Pony Club rally since she had bought Smudge. When he had first arrived he had been extremely nervous and quite naughty, and Megan was very proud of his improvement – even though he wasn't as well-schooled as the other ponies and often misbehaved.

"Before you go," continued Anna, "I want to give you some exciting news." All 12 riders sat up straighter in their saddles and listened attentively, waiting to hear what Anna had to say.

"I've been contacted by a lady who is planning to shoot a TV documentary on the Pony Club," Anna told them. "She would like to film a normal lesson but mostly she wants to concentrate on one of you, get some good shots of you riding and ask you a few questions."

> "I've been contacted by a lady who is planning to shoot a TV documentary,"

A buzz of enthusiasm passed through the riders and Megan felt sure that if they hadn't been mounted, they would have been jumping about, screaming with excitement. Anna had to wait a few minutes for them all to calm down so she could finish her announcement.

"As I said before, she really only wants to focus on one of you, so you mustn't all get your hopes up. If you're interested, which I'm sure you will be, then collect a letter from the office on the way home. The lady is going to film a lesson here in a few weeks' time, and she'll then choose one of you to interview and, hopefully, feature on the TV!"

Megan rode home with her friend Sara and Sara's brother Alex. All three of them could talk of nothing but the proposed TV documentary.

"It's going to be *such* fun," cried Sara. "I hope I'm the one who gets chosen. I doubt it'll be me, though. It'll probably be you," she said to Megan. "Smudge is so cute, they're bound to pick him."

Megan had to agree that Smudge was very sweet, but he wasn't very well behaved. "She'll never pick me," she said. "Remember how many times Smudge refused at that combination today before I finally managed to get him over it?"

"But he's had way less schooling than all the other ponies," Sara sympathised.

"Yes," agreed Megan, "but how is the lady from the television supposed to know that?"

Despite this, Megan couldn't help secretly wishing that she would be chosen. She imagined Smudge doing perfect transitions in the lesson with the TV lady watching, and then jumping all the jumps with inches to spare. Maybe he wouldn't even buck. He was doing it less and less now...

> Maybe Smudge wouldn't buck. He was doing it less and less now...

The day of the demonstration lesson finally arrived. Megan woke early. She leapt out of bed, dressed and hurried downstairs before she realised that if she went to the stables now, then Smudge would be ready much too early. Megan knew from experience that if he had to hang around waiting, he was not going to be happy. Reluctantly, she went back upstairs and spent half-an-hour trying to concentrate on a magazine, before she went to fetch Smudge in from the field.

Despite waiting, she still arrived at the Pony Club early, and found that nearly everyone else had done the same. Megan dismounted and tethered Smudge to a fence post, then went to join the others. They were all very excited, and looking much smarter than usual.

Anna seemed to notice this too, because when she arrived she raised her eyebrows and remarked, "It's nice to see you all making an effort for a change."

None of them had a chance to reply because someone yelled that they could see a van coming and they all clambered up onto the fence to catch sight of it, startling the horses grazing in the field.

It took some time for Anna to calm everyone down, but by the time the van pulled up, they were all standing beside their ponies, eagerly waiting for a glimpse of the TV crew and cameras. A tall, smiling woman with a long, blonde ponytail climbed out of the van and shook hands with Anna.

Anna turned to the riders; "Everyone, this is Melissa who is in charge of the documentary and this – she gestured to three more people who were unloading cameras and equipment from the back of the van – is the camera crew: Peter, Vicky and Simon."

Everyone mumbled a greeting. Megan felt suddenly very shy, and she could tell that she wasn't the only one. Sara, she could see, was holding on to her pony's reins much more tightly than usual.

Anna broke the awkward silence with her usual enthusiasm. "Right you lot, what are you waiting for? Let's get you all mounted and into the arena to start warming up!"

Ten minutes into the lesson Megan was feeling a lot more confident. Smudge had done some excellent canter transitions, and he hadn't bucked or spooked once. But Megan still couldn't help feeling nervous as Anna began to put up a jump in the middle of the arena. She needn't have worried; Smudge cleared it easily and Megan felt quite relaxed as she approached the jump for a second time. As soon as Smudge turned the corner towards the jump, she could tell that it was going to go wrong. Smudge was clearly over-excited; he leapt forward, his canter changed into a gallop and before Megan had a chance to stop him, he was tearing down the arena towards the jump, clearing it with a huge leap that sent Megan flying up his neck. She managed to hang on but a few seconds later Smudge came to a sudden halt and Megan tumbled over his head and onto the ground.

It wasn't a bad fall, and Megan was soon up on her feet again, but she felt mortified. Of all the times to fall off, why did it have to be in this lesson, with the TV presenter and camera crew watching? She had ruined any chances she might have had of becoming the star of the TV documentary. She spent the rest of the lesson gloomily watching the others, and wondering which of them would be chosen.

*Smudge came to a sudden halt and Megan tumbled over his head and onto the ground.*

At the end of the day, Sara and Alex wanted to stay behind and talk to Melissa, the TV presenter, so Megan rode home on her own. She felt awful. She had wanted so much to be the star of the documentary and now everything was spoiled. Smudge had been behaving so well, too. If only she hadn't tried that jump for a second time. If only she were a better rider...

*If only she hadn't tried that jump for a second time.. If only she were a better rider...*

The next day, Megan didn't feel like riding. She didn't want to go to Pony Club, either, because Anna would be announcing who the TV crew had chosen. So she stayed at home, wandering around the house doing nothing in particular. In the evening she heard her mum calling her.

"Megan! Sara's on the phone. She says she's got wonderful news for you." Megan groaned and made her way slowly downstairs. Sara must have been chosen, then. That was why she was on the phone. She would be awful at school tomorrow – gloating and rubbing it in.

Megan picked up the phone.

"Hello?"

Sara's voice at the other end sounded very excited. "Megan, you'll never guess what?" She carried on before Megan had a chance to reply. "*You've been chosen!*"

It took a few seconds for the words to sink in.

"Me?" Megan stammered. "But *how*?"

In a few minutes, Sara explained the whole story. After the disaster in the lesson, she and Alex had stayed behind to explain to Melissa how Megan had spent ages schooling Smudge and how, despite her hard work, he still wasn't as well behaved as the other ponies.

"And she was intrigued by the story," Sara said. "She's decided to change the documentary and focus on you and how you've been working with Smudge. Isn't that amazing?"

Megan was stunned into silence. She couldn't believe it. She was going to be the star of the show. At first, all she could manage to say was "Wow!" Then she realised that if Sara and Alex hadn't told Melissa the story, then she would never have been chosen. Deeply grateful, Megan thanked Sara over and over again until her embarrassed friend made some kind of excuse about having to do some homework, and said goodbye.

As soon as she had hung up the phone, Megan hurried down to the field. Smudge trotted over to the gate when he saw her, hoping for a treat. Megan wrapped her arms around her pony's soft neck and buried her face in his untidy mane.

"Thank you so much," she whispered. "You're so special."

Megan stood leaning on the field gate for a long time. Smudge was definitely not the most obedient pony. He wasn't fast or showy, but he was unique. One-in-a-million. They had been through a lot together, and even though Smudge couldn't jump a course of jumps properly, even though she fell off him regularly, Megan still valued him more than any other pony. After all, her naughty pony Smudge was a challenge. And a challenge made life a lot more exciting!

*Megan couldn't help secretly wishing she would be chosen for the documentary*

posed by models

37

# Truth or myth?

Think you know about horses and ponies? Can you separate fact from fiction? Do you dare to take our quiz and find out?

**1** Arab horses have fewer ribs than all other breeds. Truth or myth?

**2** Centaurs (half-man, half-horse) lived in the wild around 500 years ago. Truth or myth?

**3** The star constellation "The Winged Horse" is named after Pegasus because of its shape. Truth or myth?

**4** Napoleon's first horse was called Bijou. Truth or myth?

**5** Bijou pony wear is named after this horse. Truth or myth?

**6** A true dun pony will always have a dorsal stripe. Truth or myth?

**7** A chestnut mare is the worst sort of horse you can buy. Truth or myth?

**8** The hair on a zebra's stifle doesn't grow upwards like a pony's. Truth or myth?

**9** Horses can be born hairless. Truth or myth?

**10** Donkeys don't have chestnuts on their hind legs. Truth or myth?

**11** Horses can sleep standing up. Truth or myth?

**12** A mare's mane falls naturally to the right, and a gelding's to the left. Truth or myth?

**13** Feeding linseed gives ponies a shiny coat. Truth or myth?

**14** Ponies can't vomit. Truth or myth?

**15** A horse shoe on the door will bring you good luck. Truth or myth?

**16** Fell and Dales ponies are endangered species. Truth or myth?

**17** The largest mule on record was called Apollo and was a massive 19.1hh! Truth or myth?

**18** The bigger a horse's ears are, the faster he can gallop. Truth or myth?

# Answers

1 – truth, 2 – myth, 3 – myth, 4 – truth, 5 – myth, 6 – truth,
7 – myth, 8 – truth, 9 – truth, 10 – truth, 11 – truth, 12 –
myth, 13 – truth, 14 – truth, 15 – myth, 16 – truth, 17 – truth,
18 – myth, 19 – truth, 20 – truth, 21 – myth, 22 – truth

## How did you do?

### 0 - 5 right

Call yourself a pony fan? You've got some serious brushing up to do. Go out and get as many horsey books as you can get your hands on immediately!

### 6 - 11 right

Mmmmm, we're sure you can do better than that! You need to swat up and get the facts sorted from the fiction!

### 12 - 17 right

Not bad, not bad at all. Definite room for improvement, however.

### 18 - 22 right

Well done you! You can spot an old wives tale when you see one! Just remember though, you can never stop learning where ponies are concerned, and some very peculiar things often turn out to be true!

In Los Angeles, it is illegal for horses to sleep in a bakery. **Truth or myth?**

Horses with four white socks are unlucky. **Truth or myth?**

Horses have 17 muscles in each ear. **Truth or myth?**

Horses, like humans, have different blood types. **Truth or myth?**

# MAKE SOME FAB CHRISTMAS DECORATIONS!

Want to surprise your parents or friends with some fabulous handmade PONY Christmas decorations? Well, here's how to do it!

## YOU NEED:
**Needles
Glue
Stuffing
Sequins and ribbons
Gold or silver thread
Coloured thread
Scissors
Coloured felt
Pins**

## STEP ONE
Cut out the pony template on pages 98-99. Fold a piece of felt in half so that when you cut around your template, you will end up with two pony shapes.

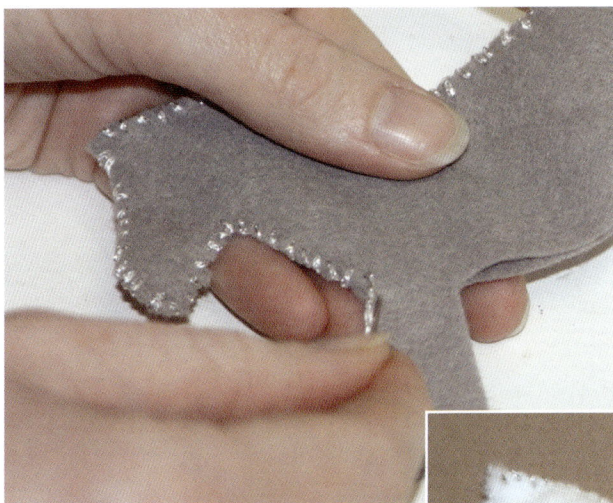

## STEP TWO
Pin the two felt shapes together and sew around the edge, leaving a small gap on the pony's belly to put the stuffing in.

## STEP THREE
Stuff the shape carefully and then sew up the gap.

## STEP FOUR
Glue on any decorations that you want on your pony, being careful not to get glue everywhere!

## TOP TIP!
Try making different pony colours — we made an appaloosa, a dappled grey, a bay and a magical unicorn!

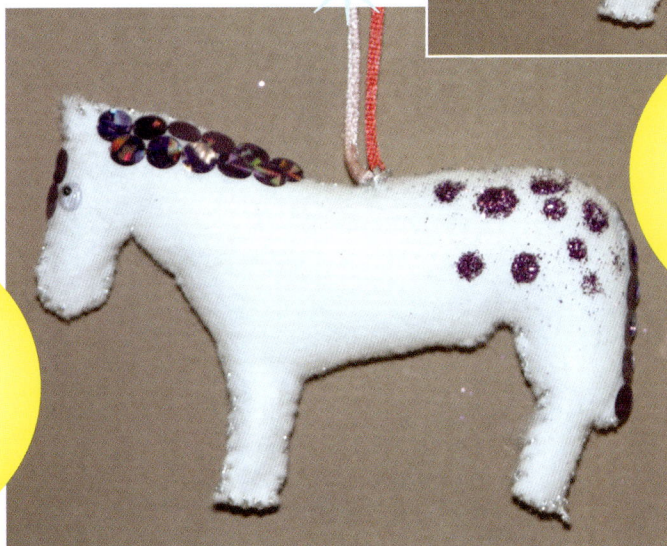

The pony template can be found on pages 98-99! Enjoy making your pony decorations!

## STEP FIVE
Sew a piece of thread through the top of your pony and knot the ends together. This will allow you to hang your decoration up!

## STEP SIX
Remember to give your pony a mane, tail and eye. We used sequins, ribbons and fun goggly eyes!

# Fabulous Fells and

These two beautiful breeds are descended from the Friesian and the Galloway pony, and their influence can still be seen in the appearance and conformation of the modern Fell and Dales ponies.

## Fell Pony Fact file

**Height:** Up to 14hh
**Colour:** Black, brown and bay. Grey is very rarely found.
**Head:** Small but well-defined.
**Type:** Hardy and coarse, but still lively, alert and of good appearance.

## What's in a name?

The first Fell pony was bred from a pony called Lingcropper, who was almost certainly a Scottish Galloway pony. He was called Lingcropper as he was discovered in 1745 eating the heather, which in Scottish can be translated to "cropping the ling".

## Map

The Pennine mountains separate the Fells from the Dales!

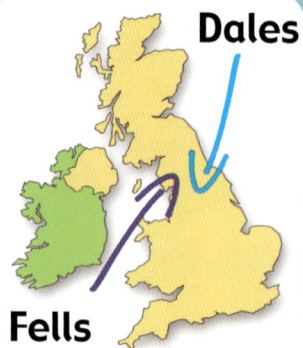

**Dales**

**Fells**

## Fabulous fact

Her Majesty the Queen owns several Fell ponies, which are used for carriage driving at Balmoral (her private Scottish holiday estate), as well being ridden by various members of the Royal Family.

## Hackney blood

Hackneys have Fell blood in their ancestry, as the Fell pony is often used to cross-breed.

## Child-friendly

The Fell pony has a lovely temperament. It is suited to all disciplines and is able to live out all year round. Keen to work, and always willing to try hard, the Fell pony makes a perfect children's pony.

# Delicious Dales

## Dales Pony Fact file

**Height:** Up to 14.2hh
**Colour:** Black, bay, grey and occasionally roan.
**Head:** Larger than Fell ponies, but still neatly put together.
**Type:** Muscular and powerful, retaining the hardiness of its ancestors.

## Marvellous miner

The Dales was often used as a pit pony, as it could pull immense weights, and was hardy enough to work for long periods of time. Like the Fell pony, it was also good under harness, and to increase its potential as a driving pony, Welsh Cob blood was introduced to the breed, via a trotting stallion called Comet, in particular.

## Did you know?

Over 200 Dales ponies were used by the army during World War I and World War II, because of their ability to carry a man all day, and because they were so strong and hardy.

## Riding away

With its combination of energy and good conformation, the Dales is a pleasure to ride. They have very good stamina and can keep going over long distances. They are therefore popular for trekking and long distance rides.

They are also brilliant jumpers and good all-rounders.

## True or false?

**1** Her Majesty the Queen owns several Fell ponies.

True ☐    False ☐

**2** The Dales pony stands up to 14.2hh.

True ☐    False ☐

**3** 75 Dales ponies were used during World War I and World War II.

True ☐    False ☐

**4** Hackneys have Fell blood in their ancestry.

True ☐    False ☐

**5** The Dales pony is often chestnut in colour.

True ☐    False ☐

**Answers**
1. True 2. True
3. False
4. True 5. False

# Celeb rider fess ups

"I was once competing in America in a major class with Locarno. We approached a jump and, instead of going over it, he decided to go under it. Unfortunately, he managed to get one of the fillers over his head and we were cantering around the ring with half of the jump on his head and neck. To make matters worse, at the after-show party, highs and lows of the event were shown on a big screen and they must have shown this incident about 10 times. I was shocked to discover that this embarrassing moment had also made the American news and was shown on the TV next day. How embarrassing!"

**Ellen Whitaker,
celeb show jumper**

**Cringe-ometer**
Filler antics!
5 4 3 2 1
**3**

"I once took part in a celebrity polo match, and as I galloped out onto the field on my smart polo pony, it put its head down and I went flying! I immediately got back on, hoping no-one had noticed, but then exactly the same thing happened again! It was really embarrassing!"

Mark Todd,
legendary event rider

**Cringe-ometer**
Polo problems!
5 4 3 2 1
**3**

"In 2006, I was having my first ride at Badminton on a horse called Arthur's Word. He produced by far his best test to date in the dressage arena, and we set out to show the world what we could do.

Unfortunately, what we did was a somersault over the bounce into the Badminton lake. We both got up fine and uninjured, but it was hugely embarrassing walking back to the stables, where every single person seemed to know me and wanted to ask what happened and if we were okay!"

Nick Gauntlett,
top event rider

**Cringe-ometer**
Silly somersault!
5 4 3 2 1
**3**

"Years ago, when I was riding my pony, Butter Boy, along the lanes where I lived, (and probably feeling a little bored!), I thought it would be a good idea to have a go at sitting behind the saddle on the pony's quarters! Butter Boy was a bit sharp, and he shot off and I fell off backwards onto the road. I ended up unconscious and had to have stitches in my head, but I never dared confess to anyone what I had been up to!"

**Mary King,
Olympic specialist**

**Cringe-ometer**
Butter fingers!
5 4 3 2 1
**4**

PONY Magazine caught up with some of our fave celebs to see what was their most embarrassing moment *ever*!

"When the Grand National is on, my friends and I go up to some local gallops that you are meant to pay for, as we know no-one will be around to spot us! Pie loves it!"
Kelly Marks, Natural Horsewoman extraordinare

**Cringe-ometer**
Sneaky galloping!
2

"Years ago, I thought I had won an advanced class at Tetbury and broke my way through the crowd to get to Princess Anne, who was presenting the prizes, only to get there, put out my hand and discover that I had not taken the top spot at all!"
Lucinda Green, eventing legend

**Cringe-ometer**
Prize disaster!
4

"When I was 10 years old, I hacked seven miles to a local show so that I could jump in the first class. Sadly, I was eliminated at the first fence, so it was a very, very long journey home!"
Tim Stockdale, jumping God

**Cringe-ometer**
Elimination error!
3

"I was riding in one of the novice classes at the East of England Show and the ground was awful. Triple X is a big, scopey stallion and he hadn't jumped on grass before and, as a result, was jumping the fences ridiculously high! I'd only jumped a few fences and was just cantering around the corner when he slipped, fell over and the next thing I knew I was on the floor! Luckily we were both unharmed, but I was left with grass stains all over the side of my breeches and a somewhat bruised pride!
I left the ring on foot and was met by my rather amused groom. We have a rule in my yard that whoever falls off has to buy the rest of the staff fresh cream cakes, so, as you can imagine, as soon as they all heard, their orders were in for me to go to the local bakers!"
Ben Maher, top show jumper

**Cringe-ometer**
Cake conundrum!
3

"A few years ago we all used to stay at Goodwood for Young Riders Training. My friend Jackie Bickley and I went out and were very late back — so much so that when I got back there was no room in the boy's dorm! Jackie sneaked me into the girl's dorm and found me a spare bed while everyone else was asleep.
The next morning though, I had to hide under the duvet while everyone else was getting up and ready, so they wouldn't know or see me — but there are quite a few competitors on the circuit now that I have seen in their PJ's and they don't even know it!"
Carl Hester, dressage guru

**Cringe-ometer**
Pyjama-drama!
4

# 6 reasons why ponymag.com rocks!

**1** PONY-fun leaping right out of your computer, cool! You're probably not allowed ponies in the house, but you can have ponymag.com!

**2** Exclusive comps – just on the webbie!

**3** Pony-tastic games to play and play and play...

**4** Shhhh, don't tell anyone! More goss from Duggie, Chaz and PONY team stars.

**5** Exclusive PONY gear you won't find anywhere else... only in the ponymag.com shop!

**6** 'Cause it's all about ponies, duh!

# How could they take my pony away?

**Melissa was overjoyed when her parents agreed to get her a pony on loan – and one she could have so much fun with. But her joy was short-lived when the owners stepped in and ruined everything...**

## A LIFE IN THE COUNTRY

Like anyone keen on anything to do with riding and ponies, I had always dreamt of having my own pony. However, my parents weren't sold on the idea, mainly because of the costs involved. We had all moved to a lovely house in the country and while we were lucky enough to own a couple of paddocks, Mum and Dad had spent a lot of money doing the house up so hadn't planned to buy me a pony!

I knew it wouldn't have been fair of me to nag them, so I didn't give it another thought – until I heard about a friend of a friend who was looking to put her lovely pony out on loan...

Natalie owned a gorgeous pony, but she didn't really get on with him. He apparently had a boisterous nature and while he sounded ideal for me – I'd been riding for years and done lots of dressage and showjumping – he was too much for Natalie to handle, she was very much a beginner. So Mum and Dad agreed that we could make a date to see him, with a view to taking him on loan.

## THE PONY FOR ME!

His name was Sparky – and that just about said it all, because he was! He was a beautiful strawberry roan with the cutest, cheekiest face – although he did have a really kind eye! I rode him in the outdoor arena and he was beautifully schooled. He behaved impeccably and seemed to be really happy that he had a job to do. Then I jumped him and he soared like a bird – it was as if we'd bonded instantly. We were made for each other, and I had no difficulty in persuading Mum and Dad that this was the pony for me! What made the loan arrangement even more special was the fact that the owners seemed really pleased we wanted him. They could see he was coming to a good, experienced home, which is what they wanted for him.

Anyway, we decided to take him on a trial period of one month and during that time, everything went well. I took Sparky to a few shows and had some good results with him, and the owners were really pleased that he seemed to be enjoying his new life. So we decided to keep him indefinitely and agreed this with the owners. I was thrilled, of course. I had already fallen in love with Sparky. In the meantime, Natalie's plan was to do lots of riding at a local equestrian centre and perhaps get another pony in a year's time. But that all went to pot...

*Sparky sounded ideal for me – we were made for each other*

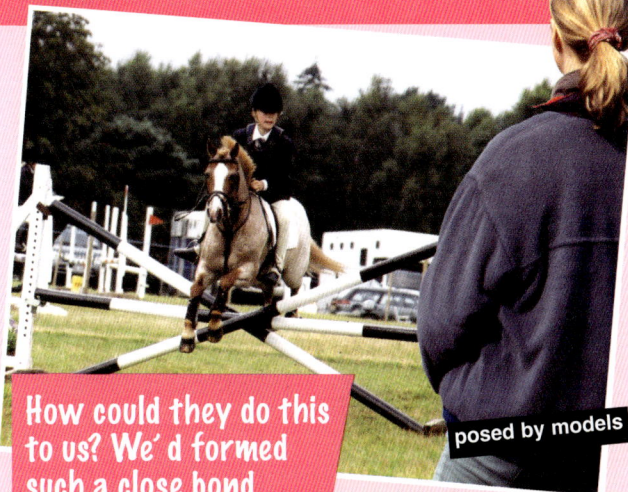

**How could they do this to us? We'd formed such a close bond**

*posed by models*

## A HUGE MISTAKE

Because we'd heard about Sparky through a friend of a friend, we hadn't bothered to draw up a proper loan agreement in writing, which turned out to be our biggest mistake ever. We had taken the owners' word when they told us they would give us plenty of notice if they ever decided they wanted Sparky back. So it came like a bolt out of the blue when they contacted us just three months later and told us that Natalie's riding had improved so much that she wanted Sparky back. And they wanted to take him away from me the following week! I was devastated – how could they do this to me and Sparky? We'd formed such a close bond and now that would be broken.

Of course, we now wish we'd drawn up a proper agreement for a stated loan time, rather than just verbally agreeing everything, just because the owners promised what we wanted to hear. It was a huge lesson to us – a very heartbreaking one – and something we'll be much more aware of in future. And now I would advise anyone thinking of taking on a loan pony to have a proper agreement in place, whether you know the owners or not.

I now see Natalie riding Sparky and being very successful with him. Don't get me wrong... I'm really pleased that her riding has come on so much, but I'm heartbroken. I am looking for another loan pony and definitely won't make the same mistake twice. We'll make sure we agree everything in writing next time – no one's going to hurt me this way again...

# PONY Mag teasers!

*How well do you know the* PONY *Mag gang? Here's a few teasers to test you – see whether you can get top marks!*

## Charlie's fiendish word puzzle

Can you solve the Charlie clues and write the answers in the spaces? The answers can be found in all the Charlie comic strips in this annual – see pages 30, 60 and 82. When you get them all right, you'll reveal the mystery word or words!

1. Charlie's sister.
2. What colour is the postman?
3. Charlie's latest girlfriend who loves art.
4. Where Charlie and his girlfriend go on a date.
5. What kind of party does Charlie go to?
6. Who is Charlene to Charlie?
7. Who's party is it?
8. What Charlie is.
9. Marilyn's surname
10. Where Charlie goes to a festival.
11. Who brings Charlie the tickets?

**The mystery word/s is/are**

....................................................

## Jorja Sudoku

Can you work out where Jigsaw, Star, CP and Raven should be so that there is one each of them in each line up-and-down, and left-to-right?

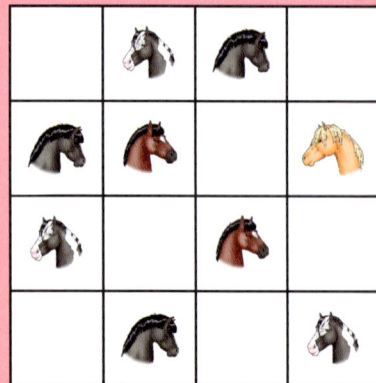

# Charlie's spot the difference

## Can you spot the five differences between picture A and picture B?

A

B

# How much of a Jorja fan are you?

**Can you spot the eight mistakes in the following passage about Jorja and her friends? See whether you're a Jorja fan or a Jorja has-been!**

Jorja

I raced to the stables today to see Jigsaw. She's my piebald cob with two wall eyes and she lives between CP, who belongs to Matt, and Star, Molly's black gelding. CP is a chestnut with a flaxen mane and tail and Matt rides him like a cowboy. Star is a bit of a maniac and is always throwing a wobbler – but Molly's got the measure of him. He's called Star because he has a lovely white star on his forehead. He's a bit mad, though.

Anyway, when I got there, Molly was grooming Star with a worn-out dandy brush – she never takes care of her things – and Matt was talking to Angelina, his on-off girlfriend.

"Hi Jorja," said Angelina, brushing her short blond hair away from her face. "Are you going riding today?"

"Yes," I replied, "Molly and I are going on one of Catherine's lessons today." Catherine owns the stables, Marsh Farm, where we keep our ponies.

Molly

"I'm riding CP," said Angelina. Matt's playing football." Football is Matt's other love – CP is his first.

"I wish you could find CP's noseband, Matt," grumbled Angelina. "He looks so naked without it.

"He never has his noseband on – he loves that look!" said Matt.

Matt

"Would anyone like a *Malteser*?" Molly asked. She's always eating chocolate.

"Yes please!" we all chorused, diving into the bag and stuffing ourselves.

# Duggie's true or false?

**Which of the following statements about Duggie, Colonel and Soloman are true, and which are false?**

1. Duggie and Soloman are New Forest ponies. True ☐ False ☐

2. Colonel is a mini Shetland pony. True ☐ False ☐

3. Soloman has a white patch on his off side flank. True ☐ False ☐

4. Duggie hates jumping. True ☐ False ☐

5. Duggie is nine years old. True ☐ False ☐

6. Duggie's full show name is Lakeview Knight. True ☐ False ☐

It's the Duggster!

Cutie Colonel

Sensible Soloman

49

# Clear round countdown!

You'll get a clear round every time if you follow our fab clear round countdown!

**6** Ride around the arena and get your bearings – listen out for the start bell.

**5** Once the bell goes, approach your first jump so you meet it perfectly, and ride positively. Look over to your next jump.

**10** Enter a class suitable for your and your pony's experience. No-one starts with the Hickstead Derby!

**9** Make sure your pony is prepared for show jumps. He should be confident jumping uprights, spreads, doubles and trebles, as well as being confident with fillers and brightly painted poles and planks.

**4**

according to your plan. Stay focused and give your pony every chance to jump well.

**3**

Ride through the finish and let your pony pull up slowly. You'll want to give him a pat!

**2**

Walk your pony around to cool him down.

**1**

If you're in the jump off (and you should be!), then you'll need to do it all over again!

**8**

Walk the course. Make sure you know the way and plan your turns so that you give your pony every chance of jumping clear. Don't rush this bit – it will pay off when it's your turn to jump.

**7**

Warm up wisely. Jumping the practice jump over and over again doesn't warm-up your pony – it wears him out!
    Here's a plan:
● **Find out when you're due to jump** so you can plan your warm-up.
● Decide how much warming up your pony needs.
● **Get your pony going forward and listening to you.**
● Jump a few jumps to get him 'in the mood.'
● **Plan your entry into the ring** so that your pony is cantering in good, bouncy strides.

You can find these counters on page 99 to cut out!

**6**

Me and Colonel stop for a cuddle, ahhh – miss your next go.

**7**

**8**

Charlie gets active on the trampoline – move forward three spaces.

I deeply object to being dragged along when doing in-hand showing classes – move back two spaces!

**4**

**3**

# Duggie's ra

Me and Colonel go for a gallop around the field – move forward two spaces!

**2**

Me and Soloman go for a lovely hack – go forward one space.

**1 Start**

**23**

**22**

Charlie chills in the sun – move back one space.

**24**

I stop for a snooze – your next

**Finish!**

**25**

**21**

**26**

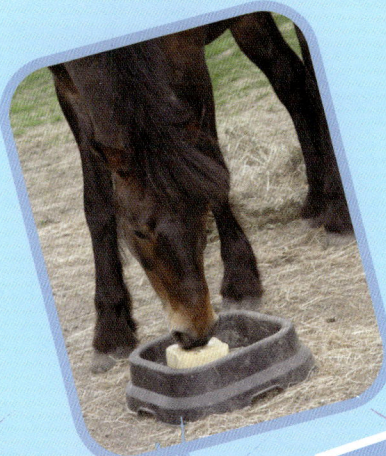

**10**

Soloman finds a tasty treat to munch on – move forward one space.

**11**

**12**

I'm made to have a bath – go back one space!

**13**

I get a lovely groom – move forward one space.

# e for home!

**Welcome to my game 'Race for home'! Play with your friends and see who can get back to the field first. But beware – there are tricks and temptations along the way!**

**14**

Colonel stops for a scratch – miss your next go.

**15**

I let myself out of my stable and go for a wander – move forward three spaces!

**16**

## How to play:

- This game is for two – four players. Cut out the counters and decide who will be who.
- You'll need a dice. Take it in turns to roll the dice and move around the board.
- If you land on one of the special spaces, you must do what it tells you to!
- First one back to the field is the winner!

**17**

and Soloman
ake friends
ain – move
rward two
spaces.

**20**

Me and Soloman have a row – move back one space!

**18**

**19**

# War drums

## By PONY reader Heather Farmer

**Many stories have been told of man and his horse in battle. Great descriptions of fair warriors atop fiery steeds with flared nostrils and flaming eyes, pawing the ground in anticipation. Maybe there is truth in these stories, but from my experience I have serious doubts. The life of a war horse is far from grand.**

I suppose I should start with who I am. I was born near London on a stately stud farm, sired by Wersaw out of Fallowed Nights, both strong Thoroughbred horses. I never met my father, but my mother told me that he had been a great horse in the British Army. His legacy was to be continued by me, although I did not know this. I was just a young colt with a glossy, liver chestnut coat and rich, dark eyes. My innocence ended when I was just two. I was taken from my home and transported with many others to the British Cavalry Barracks, an enormous place with many schools and hundreds of stables. I was put in stall 56, between a young grey who neighed all night, and a bad tempered bay, who tried to bite me through the intersecting rails. It was a sad night, but I was excited. I knew where I was and looked forward to finding out more about my new life.

The barracks became my home and life, and for several years I trained and mastered all sorts of challenges. By now I was a handsome 16hh gelding by the name of Drummer Boy, though many of the men referred to me as Calm Wersaw — apparently, my father had been a highly-strung version of me! But, in 1914, my life changed forever when I truly began to walk in my father's footsteps during World War One.

The first we knew of the War was the frenzied activity of the stable hands cleaning out disused stables, and the bellowing orders from the sergeants to spring clean the human living quarters. Over the next month, hundreds of young men, newly signed up to the army, flooded onto the site and extra horses from all over the country were seen rearing in the schools. Thus began the training for war.

Though we had been taught to ride on while our soldier took aim, and not flinch when bullets flew past our ears, the technology we experienced now was more terrifying than you could ever imagine. Hand-held explosives were flung through the air to blast the ground before us to smithereens, and the constant clatter of machine gun fire made our heads ache. If they ever made it to the arena, the tanks scared us witless, clanking and groaning like monstrous beasts. But by far the worst were things we referred to as High Howlers (the men called them bombs or shells), flung from behind the soldiers, high into the air. When they landed they made craters the size of two horses, destroying everything in one foul blast.

> **"Hand-held explosives were flung through the air to blast the ground before us to smithereens, and the constant clatter of machine gun fire made our heads ache."**

The men, too, were alien — no more careful soldiers for us. In all fairness, they tried their hardest to remember all the information, but it takes years to remember, learn and conquer all the techniques needed — they only had months. Many times I had to be ridden with reins around my knees and the wrong saddle pinching my back. It was not unknown either to have your saddle taken off and be left without water, rug or clean coat, just abandoned. You were lucky to get a rider who had sat on a donkey at a fair, let alone someone with any knowledge, and that was when people had time to tack up and groom. That luxury wasn't there on the battle field, something that I would soon find out.

We were shipped to France in huge, smelly boats that screamed and tossed in the waves. Many of the young horses never made it there. This was my first image of death, as they had to be put down so as to not sink the boat. When we arrived we were confronted by strange sights and smells, but my training to 'just keep going' helped me, especially over the coming weeks which were spent journeying to our destination — our first battle. We didn't really understand who or what we were meant to be fighting, but there was a definite sense of excitement and even impatience to get there. After all, I for one had been training all of my life for this.

I don't remember much of what happened next, all I know is that the sudden flurry and yelling heralded one of the worst moments of my life. Our scouts had come with the news that a battle to our west had gone drastically downhill and they needed emergency assistance. Next moment, we were saddled for war and cantering blindly towards a far away roar. The foot soldiers in our group were following but as we were faster, the cavalry was sent on ahead. About 200 strong, we charged straight into the enemy flanks and in less than three seconds we went down. I stared in horror as my fellows fell to the power of the enemy guns, as my rider screamed at me to move on. He aimed his rifle at a man and fired, but I couldn't watch. I stumbled blindly into the fray, watching through wide eyes as lives were snuffed out like candles. It was over soon, our side took the advantage and the enemy retreated. The men began to celebrate their win but we, the horses, just stood staring at that which we had spent all our

ves preparing for. '*What have I done?*' is all I could think.

But there was no point thinking, as I knew this was what life was going to be from now on, whether I liked it or not. I allowed myself to be led to an open area where all the horses were picketed, and we ate in subdued silence. We found out later that the men intended to stay here for what sounded like a long time.

When I say the enemy retreated, I didn't mean they ran away never to be seen again. Oh no, in the First World War there was something

called *the trench system* which the men fought from. Basically, we had lots of ditches and trenches on our side which the men fired from, an area of land in the middle, known as *No Man's Land* — and then the enemy had the same sort of trenches on the other side. It was all about gaining land, so the army had to run across *No Man's Land* to get to the enemy trenches. When they got there, if there were enough of them, they would

take over the trench and the enemy would have to fall back to their second set of trenches. It wasn't that easy to get across though, with machine guns and High Howlers dropping on you, but it still seemed very important to the men to get there, no matter how much was lost in the attempt. The other horses and I couldn't understand it at all.

My second battle was as bad as the first. We were sent out with a wave of foot soldiers to try and cross *No Man's Land*. We charged across the wasteland, having been driven into a frenzy by the sergeants. I remember galloping out beside my friends and watching as the enemy did the same, and their machine guns started to fire. It was a horrific affair, with High Howlers exploding and people screaming. The man on my back suddenly gasped and I felt him fall.

Spinning around, I saw him crumpled in death upon the grassless ground. My fellows charged away as the battle swung to the east, but I could not leave. I had been trained to stay by my rider's side, but in that wasteland alone, with High Howlers dropping like rain, my nerve broke. Horses don't stay and fight, they take flight, though as I pranced and foamed at the mouth, I knew there was nowhere to run to. Then I spotted a man coming towards me. He was running, waving his arms and shouting. Behind him I saw his horse on the ground.

"Get 'ere," the man shouted, grabbing my reins.

I snorted, rearing away. The man looked mad.

"No," I screamed. "Get back, get away from me!"

I pawed the ground, flattening my ears, but for all the good it did, I might as well have laid down for him to mount. I wasn't strong enough to stop him, my nature forbade me and he knew it. I was forced again into battle.

We lost so many lives that day. I remember limping back to the field where we slept. I had been hit in the shoulder by a shard of metal blasted from a High Howler, only to find less than half of our number huddled up, shivering. I went over to my friend, Shaman's Call, a tough little Arabian horse, who was quaking in her shoes.

"I thought you were dead," she said, touching her nose to mine.

"Not yet," I replied, as cheerfully as I could manage, though she heard the pain in my voice. She whickered quietly to me, grooming my back as I groomed hers. Another friend, Justique, a French horse, said:

"They won't let you ride for a while with that wound — lucky." He was right, I did miss the next few battles, but that only made it worse when they came back, every time with a few more lost. The men were given kind words and comfort for their misery, but we received nothing. They didn't care for our sanity. No-one thought of us when we saw someone blown to pieces. No-one remembered that we had eaten opposite the horse which they were now dragging past dead. No-one remembered to console us about the horse that we had groomed an hour before. No-one thought of the comradeship formed between two horses who had stood side by side, swishing flies off each others faces with their tails. No. Not a word.

Only one man ever mentioned it to me, and that was more for his benefit than mine.

"No worries mate," he said, trembling as he yanked on my bridle. "If yer die 'ere, yer go to nice pastures of sweet grass. And I'll go to heaven, I will." He grinned lopsidedly at me, pulling out a tatty little book from his jerkin pocket.

"God will save us," he said "Or we'll go to a better place."

'Wouldn't be hard,' I thought as he wrenched up my girth. 'Just need to knock some sense into the humans so we can get away from here.' But I did feel ashamed of this when I heard a Sergeant say that 'Bible Boy' had been shot down. I hope he went where he wanted to go.

But it was true. As I stood with Justique after yet another fight, mourning the loss of my beautiful Shaman's Call who had gone down so bravely, I felt a flare of anger towards the humans. I could not understand them. Why were they so eager to destroy one another? There was no sense in their killing. We understand that some animals have to hunt to eat, but never just for... for what?

**Maybe there was a reason, but I never found it. We used to call to the enemy horses from across the wasteland man had created. They were the same as us, and their owners did the same things. There was nothing different about them, except that they were on the other side, though what defined this we were never told. Thinking back, we were never told anything, yet we were expected to carry on at all costs. Perhaps they thought we were just dumb animals, but you know better, don't you?**

# The A – Z of horses

## N is for...

**Napping** – when a pony is reluctant to leave home and refuses to go forward when asked.

**Navicular disease** – a serious condition where the navicular bone in the foot becomes rough and pitted, and rubs against the deep digital flexor tendon, causing great pain. It is a degenerative condition for which there is no cure, and is almost always found in the front feet.

**Numnah** – the pad that goes under the saddle to offer cushioning and protection.

## O is for...

**On the bit** – the term used when a pony's head is in the vertical position when being ridden. The rest of the body must be supple and relaxed for the pony to be working in a true and correct outline.

**Over-reach** – when the toe of the hind foot strikes the heel of the front foot causing an injury. Over-reach boots are used to protect against this.

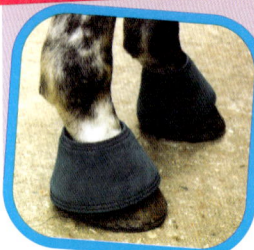

## P is for...

**Pastern** – the area between the hoof and the fetlock.

**Pelham bit** – designed to have a similar action to a double bridle, but it is one bit used with two reins.

## Pigeon-toed

**Pigeon-toed** – a conformational fault where the hooves turn inwards.

**Puissance** – a showjumping competition with a huge fence (usually a wall) that may go higher than two metres and 10 cms!

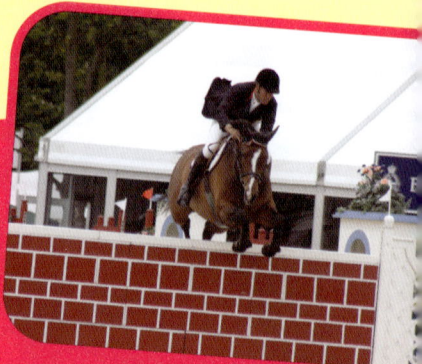

## Q is for...

**Quidding** – when a pony drops or sprinkles his food on the floor when he chews. This usually happens if the horse has an injury in the mouth or with old ponies that have lost some teeth!

**Quartering** – grooming whilst keeping a pony's rug on and folded up to expose the area you want to brush. Keeps him nice and toasty when it's cold!

## R is for...

**Ragwort** – a common wildflower with yellow petals that is poisonous to horses. It spreads very quickly in fields and must be dug up from the root and burnt.

**Rain scald** – a bacterial infection, similar to mud fever, which occurs on the body.

**Rein-back** – a school movement where you ask the horse to move backwards two or three steps.

**Ringworm** – a very contagious fungal disease. You'll see raised, circular spots where the coat will eventually fall out. It requires immediate isolation and treatment.

**Roman nose** – a convex shaped head, often seen in heavy horse breeds.

# and ponies!

## S is for...

*Seedy toe* – a condition where the hoof wall separates from the sensitive internal tissue of the hoof. Dirt and muck is then able to get inside and cause an infection.

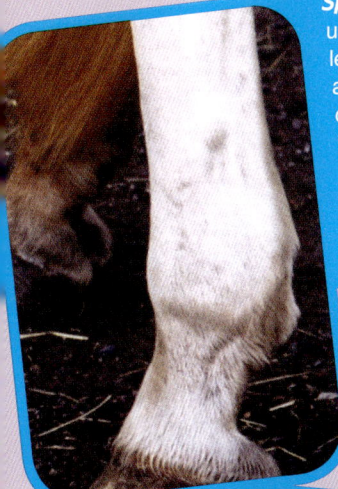

*Splint* – a bony growth, usually found on a front leg between the cannon and splint bone. Usually occurs in young horses from a knock, or concussion from overworking. Once formed, they don't usually cause a problem, except as a blemish on show ponies.

*Studs* – screwed into specially designed shoes to give horses better grip, especially when jumping.

*Sweet itch* – mostly occurring in the summer, it is a horrible condition. Ponies affected are bitten by midges and have an allergic reaction to them. It makes them very itchy and ponies can get very distressed by it.

## T is for...

*Thoroughpin* – a swelling on either side of the hock that occurs due to overwork.

*Thrush* – a horrid condition of the hooves that comes about from ponies standing in wet and dirty conditions. It makes the frog soft, squidgy and really smelly!

*Tubbing* – used to treat foot problems. The horse's foot is placed in a plastic or rubber bucket filled with warm water and maybe salts.

## U is for...

*Unbroken* – a horse or pony that has never been ridden.

## V is for...

*Vaulting* – a fun and exciting discipline which is a bit like gymnastics on horseback!

## W is for...

*Weaving* – a vice where ponies swing their head and neck from side-to-side, usually in their stable. They shift weight from one front foot to the other causing, them to lose condition.

*Windgall* – a fluid swelling around the fetlock area.

## X, Y and Z are for...

*X* – marks the centre of a school or arena.

*Yearling* – a one-year-old horse or pony.

*Zebra marks* – Stripes found on the legs of some breeds, such as Highland ponies.

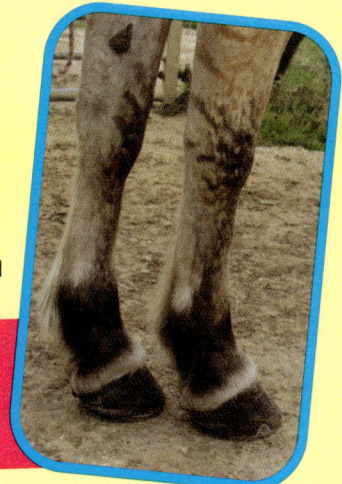

Being a true friend to the pony in your life isn't always easy – there will be times when your friendship will be tested. So how do you score as a pony friend? Be totally honest...

**1 You go out to catch your pony from his field, and he runs away. Do you:**

a) Chase after him until he tires out and gives up?

b) Shout at him because he is wasting your time?

c) Wonder what is wrong, as he's usually easy to catch, and entice him in with some treats.

**2 You and your mates have set out on a picnic ride. The pony you are riding feels a little unsound. Do you:**

a) Return to the stables – even though you have been looking forward to this special day for ages.

b) Carry on, but spend the entire ride worrying about it.

c) Ignore it, and chat and giggle with your friends.

**3 A friend invites you over after school to try out her latest DS game, but your pony needs his tea. Do you:**

a) Tell yourself he won't miss one meal too much, and go off to your friend's house?

b) Go back to your friend's house, and keep on thinking you should have gone to feed your pony?

c) Explain to your friend why you can't go home with her, but suggest you sort something out for the weekend?

**4 Your pony is sweaty after your hack. You know you should get him dried off before you turn him out with his rug on because the weather is cold – but you are dying to go back home to watch Hannah Montana. Do you:**

a) Put him out in the field with his turnout rug on, hoping that the sweat will dry out in the end.

b) Wait for your pony to dry off before rugging up, and call your mum and ask her to record your programme.

c) Put him out with no rug on.

**5 You are competing in a showjumping class at your local show and the pony you are riding knocks lots of jumps down. Do you:**

a) Put a brave face on it, and tell him he tried his best.

b) Give him a good crack with the whip so he knows he has been naughty.

c) Burst into tears because you can't bear everyone thinking you're not much good at riding.

**6 You're out on a hack with a lush boy you are desperately trying to impress, and all he wants to do is gallop. Do you:**

a) Go along with it, and return back to the yard with hot, sweaty, puffed-out ponies.

b) Tell him you'll take a short cut and meet him at the end of the track so he can have another good gallop.

c) Try to get it into his head that constant galloping isn't exactly good for the ponies' legs.

**7 The acorns are starting to drop from the oak tree in your pony's field. Do you:**

a) Pick them up daily, to make sure that there is no chance of your pony eating them and getting colic.

b) Pick them up from time-to-time, hoping that none has been eaten.

c) Tell yourself that your pony won't eat them, so there is no risk.

**8** You've turned up for your weekly lesson on your fave riding school pony, and the instructor tells you that he is injured, so has organised for another pony for you to ride. Do you:
a) Throw a tantrum because you don't want to ride any other pony than Snowy.
b) Get your mum to complain to the teacher.
c) Say Hi to Snowy and then get on with the lesson on Soldier.

**9** You're on a riding holiday, and you are afraid to admit that you don't know how to put a bridle on, so you bash the bit into your pony's mouth to get him to open it. Do you:
a) 'Fess up and ask your teacher to show you the right way to do it.
b) Keep on doing it the wrong way as it is too embarrassing to admit to being a failure.
c) Ram the bit in his mouth to teach him a lesson.

**10** You have outgrown your pony, but you can't bear to be parted from him as you love him to bits. Do you:
a) Keep on riding him, despite being too big for him.
b) Get cross with him for not growing bigger with you.
c) Talk to your parents about the best way to find a really good, loving home for him.

## SO HOW DO YOU SCORE AS A FRIEND TO YOUR FAVE PONY? CHECK OUT THE ANSWERS BELOW!

1-C; 2-A; 3-C; 4-B; 5-A; 6-C; 7-A; 8-C; 9-A; 10-C

### True friend – 10-10
You are a true friend! Whatever happens, you will put your own interests behind the needs of your fave pony. It's not an easy thing to do, so well done you!

### Pretty good friend – 7-10
Most of the time, you are a good mate, but you just slip on the odd occasion. With a bit more thought, you could soon hit the highly desirable 10 out of 10 mark!

### Pretty poor friend – 4-7
There are too many other things you want to do, so putting your fave pony first doesn't happen all that often. You need to think hard about your priorities.

### Not a friend at all – 0-4
You've got a lot of hard work to do, and some serious thinking, if you want to carry on with ponies. Maybe they need more of your love and commitment than you are currently prepared to give?

# CHARLIE GOES TO GLASTONBURY!

Yes, result! I can't *believe* we got Glastonbury tickets!

I told you we would guys... rock on the summer!

Are the tickets here yet Mum?

No, not yet Charlie.

What if they don't come in time?

Charlie, it's still a month away!

Yes, the postman's here! He must have the tickets today!

I think this might be what you're waiting for, Charlie.

My Glastonbury tickets!

Hey guys, the Glastonbury tickets came through this morning!

Excellent!

I can't believe it's raining, what a nightmare!

I know, I'm taking my waterproofs and wellies!

Guys, don't panic! The forecast says it's going to brighten up.

See guys, I told you the weather would be good!

Well I'm taking my wellies just to be on the safe side.

Me too, I don't want to get covered in mud if it does rain!

Wellies, pah! You won't need those guys. More like sun cream and a straw hat!

I can't believe you two have brought so much stuff, all you need is a few t-shirts and shorts!

I've got waterproof and warm clothes in case the weather turns.

It won't, I'm telling you!

Shades, check. Straw hat, check. Come on you two, let's go!

You two look ridiculous!

Charlie, have you not seen that big rain cloud coming over?

I'm sure it will just be a quick and refreshing shower then it'll pass...

What did we tell you! Everyone knows it always rains at Glastonbury!

Come on Charlie, we better see if we can buy you some clothes!

Is this really all you could find!

I'm afraid so!

Well at least you'll be warm and dry now!

# I can't let him go

**Joey was Amelia's first pony and he turned out to be the best ever! But one day the vet told her something she dreaded to hear. What would she do?**

## DREAM COME TRUE

When Mum and Dad bought me my beloved Dartmoor pony, Joey, I was thrilled, vowing that I would never part with him, come what may. I had waited so long for a pony of my own and Joey was going to be my best friend, ever. I was totally in love.

Joey and I bonded right from the start. He loved all the fuss I made of him and he seemed to enjoy all the things we did together – hacking, gymkhanas, sponsored rides with Mum on her horse, and just general things like being groomed and cuddled. It all seemed a far cry from the life he'd had before as a companion pony to a competition showjumper. He'd been well-looked after, but the owners never had much time to pamper and spoil him. Now, however, it was a different story – he shared a paddock with Mum's mare and had his own cosy stable!

*The vet shook his head and I felt fear stab at my heart.*

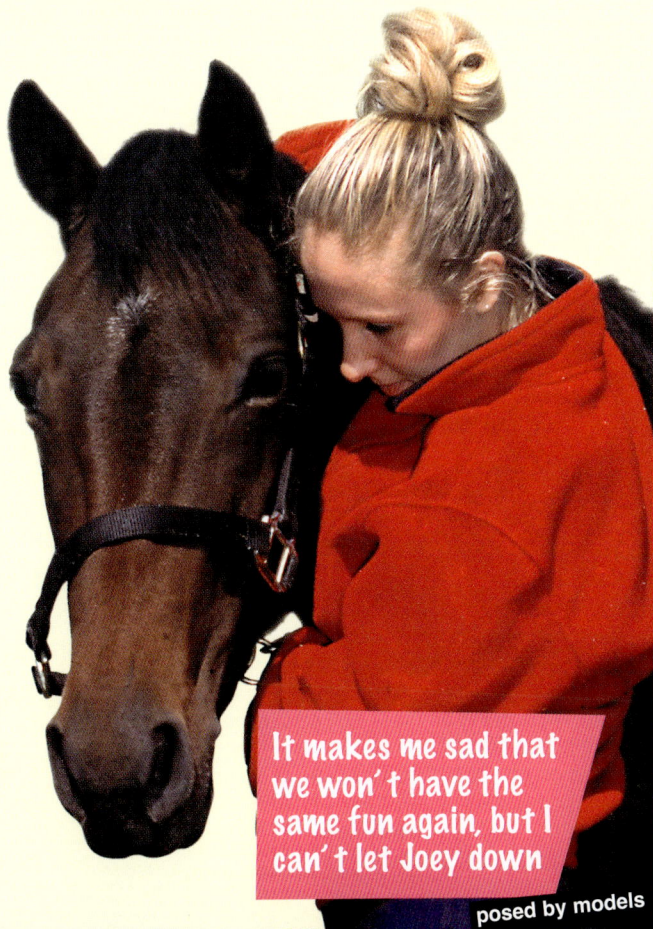

## NOT ALL GOOD NEWS...

Joey was 16 years old, so had seen a bit of the world and was very experienced. He was great in traffic, very well-mannered and a great jumper, so everything I could want in a first pony. He also gave me loads of confidence, especially when I started jumping. And he was as fit as a fiddle, except for an old niggly injury to a fetlock joint in one of his front legs. He was a bit arthritic in that leg and sometimes went a bit hoppy on it, but my vet assured me he wasn't in any pain.

Joey's little 'war wound' didn't seem to bother him in the summer when it was warm – only during the colder months of winter. And then, of course, as he got older, it started to bother him more – and instead of being occasionally hoppy on it, he was beginning to get more and more lame. The vet checked him out regularly, and we always thought the diagnosis would be the same as before – nothing to worry about.

## THE WORST DAY EVER

Then came a day I'll never forget. Joey went lame, and after a week when he didn't get any better, we called out the vet as a matter of course. Only this time, the vet didn't say Joey would be fine. This time, the shook his head and I felt fear stab at my heart. The stresses of being ridden were putting too much pressure on poor Joey's injured joint. I was devastated... We don't have enough land to keep any more horses, so my parents told me I would either have to get rid of Joey and get a new pony, or keep him, even though I can never ride him again.

I could never get rid of Joey – even if he was unrideable. Some of my friends think I'm mad to keep a pony I can't ride but Joey's very happy out with Mum's horse, and he still loves being fussed over! It's as though he's grateful to me for keeping him.

## FRIEND FOR LIFE

Joey has been such a great friend and confidence giver that the least we can do for him is look after him in his old age. Besides, I love him too much to part with him, as does the rest of the family. And my friends don't really understand the bond we have – we're like two peas in a pod, character-wise. The only difference is that he's got four legs and I've got two! We still have fun together, we just don't go riding anymore..

I do remember the good times we had together and it makes me sad that we won't have the same fun again. But then, I've been lucky to have had those happy times in the first place. And anyway, Joey trusts me, so I can't let him down – just as he has never let me down.

*It makes me sad that we won't have the same fun again, but I can't let Joey down*

posed by models

61

# Cool Cama

## Fact file

**Height:** 14hh

**Colour:** Always grey

**Build:** strong back, but with flat withers. The head is heavy and coarse.

**Characteristics:** free-roaming on the Rhone Delta in France, the Camargue is built to withstand varying weather conditions, and food intake.

## Cave drawings

The Camargue is an ancient breed, which bears a strong resemblance to the cave drawings found at Lascaux and Niaux, dated 15,000 BC. This suggests that the Camargue horse has been around Southern France since prehistoric times.

## Nature reserve

Most of the Camargue has now been drained in order to grow rice and vines, but the horses are still used to drive bulls, as well as being used in the tourist industry, to allow people to see the Camargue nature reserve from horseback.

People going on these riding holidays get to ride actual Camargue horses around the nature reserve here on a sort of horseback safari, and as I'm sure you will agree, there is no better way of watching beautiful wildlife than from horseback!

# rgues

Known as the horses of the sea, Camargues are hardy, strong and able to withstand their extreme environment.

## Walk the walk

The Camargue horses have a distinctive high-stepping walk, but their trot is very short and choppy. The canter and gallop are free-moving and fast, so more often than not, Camargues are ridden at this speed.

## Branding irons

In order to identify them easily, Camargue horses are branded on their near-side quarters.

## Yee-hah!

Camargue horses are often used for rounding up the black bulls which also live on the Rhone Delta. Ridden by French cowboys, known as gardians, the horses work as instinctively as sheepdogs herding sheep, and have the courage to send the bulls in the right direction.

The gardians use a saddle similar to those found in Iberia. The saddle has a deep seat with cage stirrups, and allows the gardians to ride for long periods of time, as well as supporting the rider's seat.

## Quick-fire quiz

Look at the following questions and say the first answer that comes into your head, then check it against the answers to see if you were right! You can also challenge a friend, and see who can get the most correct!

**1** What are Camargue horses also known as?

**2** Where in the world can you find Camargue horses?

**3** What paces are Camargue horses often ridden at?

**4** What is special about the way Camargue horses walk?

**5** What animals are often rounded up using Camargue horses?

## Origins

The Camargue horse comes from the Rhone Delta in Southern France. It is a harsh area to live in, fiercely hot in summer and covered with cold, salt water the rest of the year. The Camargue horses are known as *the horses of the sea*.

## The Camargue

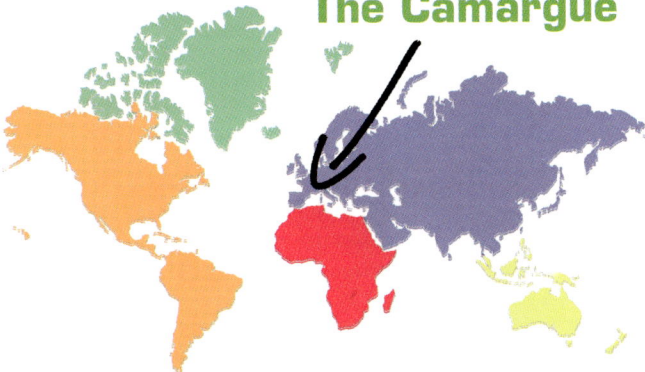

*Answers*
1. The Camargue horses are also known as *the horses of the sea*.
2. In the Rhone Delta, which is found in Southern France.
3. The Camargue is often ridden at a canter or gallop.
4. The Camargue horses have a very high-stepping walk.
5. The black bulls of the Rhone Delta.

63

# What's your star sign destiny?

Check out your star sign to discover your pony destiny. It's written in the stars!

## Capricorn (Dec 22 – Jan 20)

Capricorns love all the hard work involved in looking after their fave pony. But beware – you could find others on the yard leaving all their dirty jobs for you to do!

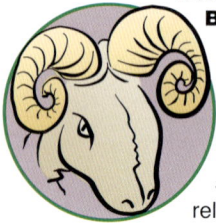

**Fave pony pastime:** Making sure the yard is spick and span. You can't relax until it's spotless!

**Best pony career:** You'd make a great groom – your horses would be the best-turned out at all the shows!

*What's in store for you and your friends?*

## Aquarius (Jan 21 – Feb 18)

You're a bit of a pony swot – you love learning all you can about horses and ponies. You're the person everyone wants on their quiz team, you know so much!

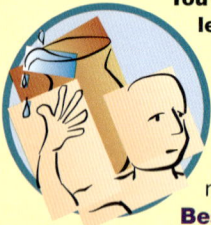

**Fave pony pastime:** Reading your pony care books. Remember to go riding now and again!

**Best pony career:** A lecturer at an equine college would be fab for you – you'll get a chance to put all that swotting up to a good use!

## Aries (Mar 20 – April 19)

You love to be in charge – you just can't help it! If there's something to organise, you'll be the one to do it, but remember that your fave pony might like to have an opinion sometimes, too!

**Fave pony pastime:** Talking about ponies! If you can find someone who shows an interest, you'll talk all day!

**Best pony career:** If you could be a head girl in a riding school or livery yard, you'd be in heaven!

## Pisces (Feb 19 – Mar 19)

Pisceans love helping others and are quite artistic. You are passionate about ponies, and hate to read about them being mistreated in any way.

**Fave pony pastime:** Drawing and painting your fave pony – it's in the stars!

**Best pony career:** Working for an equine charity would be perfect for you!

## Taurus (Apr 20 – May 20)

Taurians don't like to share, so if you ride at a riding school, you could find it difficult to share your fave pony. But you are brilliant at making him feel really special.

**Fave pony pastime:** Grooming your favourite pony is something you'd never tire of. It's a great way to bond with him, too.

**Best pony career:** A career where you can bond with your pony is right for you. You could be a famous dressage rider and reach for the stars!

*Leos are as brave as a lion*

*Taureans love to groom their fave ponies*

## Gemini (May 21 – Jun 20)

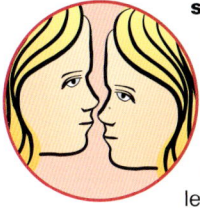

Geminis can multi-task like anything, so you're the one who's mucking out, filling a water bucket and remembering a dressage test – all at the same time!

**Fave pony pastime:** A riding lesson is your idea of horsey heaven. You love to learn all you can.

**Best pony career:** You'd make fabulous yard secretary as you can juggle so many important decisions and tasks at once.

## Cancer (Jun 21 – Jul 22)

You're a homemaker, so you're great at making your fave pony's stable the envy of all the other ponies on the yard. Go easy on the stable decorations, though, ponies aren't great art-lovers!

**Fave pony pastime:** You're ace at listening to your friends' riding problems and helping them to solve them.

**Best pony career:** Life as a riding instructor would be brilliant for you! You notice things, and can work out how best to help your pupils.

## Leo (Jul 23 – Aug 22)

Your sign is a lion, and Leos are as brave as their sign! You're up for anything when you're in the saddle, so a competitive life is for you!

**Fave pony pastime:** Anything which requires courage and a dash of recklessness. Careful, though – your pony may not be as brave as you!

**Best pony career:** You're destined to be a three-day eventer or a famous showjumper. You're not afraid to take risks to reach the top!

## Virgo (Aug 23 – Sep 22)

You love order and you're always writing lists. You do everything really well, and love everything about ponies – from looking after them to riding.

**Fave pony pastime:** You love making sure everything is in its place. Your grooming kit is an inspiration!

**Best pony career:** You're a caring sign, so a career as a veterinary nurse would be the perfect job for you.

Librans love to analyse their riding

## Libra (Sep 23 – Oct 22)

Librans enjoy working things out, so you're ace at solving pony puzzles, as well as analysing your riding.

**Fave pony pastime:** You love nothing more than just gazing at your fave pony as he grazes in the field.

**Best pony career:** Your enquiring nature is certain to make you a great equine journalist.

## Scorpio (Oct 23 – Nov 21)

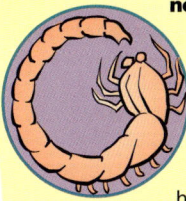

Solving mysteries is your thing, so you think nothing of riding new and difficult ponies, and getting the best out of each one of them.

**Fave pony pastime:** Pushing boundaries is your idea of fun – why not try something different. Side saddle might be the challenge for you!

**Best pony career:** A career training horses is the one for you!

## Sagittarius (Nov 22 – Dec 21)

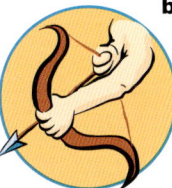

You love to travel and can't bear to be bored so trying different horsey skills is your idea of fun.

**Fave pony pastime:** Anything new – driving, polocrosse, horseball – it's all out there!

**Best pony career:** A career with horses abroad would suit you, or a travelling groom. You'd love to see the world!

What will you try next?

## Stroller

Imagine a *pony* competing against the world's best in the Olympics! If you don't think it could be possible, you're wrong! It did happen in the shape of an amazing 14.2hh pony called Stroller, ridden and owned by Marion Mould. When Stroller won a silver medal in the 1968 Mexico City Olympics, he captured the heart of the nation.

The year before Mexico, Stroller won the Hickstead Derby, the only pony to ever have won this event. He won, in total, 61 major international competitions, and lived to the ripe old age of 36 after 15 years of happy retirement.

## Ryan's Son

One of the great characters on the showjumping circuit, everyone loved this big-hearted horse's habit of bucking after the last fence in the ring. He looked like a Clydesdale crossed with a Thoroughbred and was, for 10 years, the biggest money-winner on the circuit. With his brilliant rider John Whitaker, he won at all the big international events and was an Olympic silver medallist.

His sudden death at Hicksead, at the age of 18 in 1987, was a terrible shock – not just for those who were close to him, but to his huge number of fans around the world.

## Milton

John Whitaker, whose brilliant partnership with Milton brought success after success, once said about this gorgeous grey horse, that he was 'simply the best'! Milton became the first horse outside the racing world to win more than £1million in prize money and had a string of silver and gold medals at international competitions to his name.

A great favourite with the crowd, throughout his career Milton rarely touched a rail or refused a fence. He often ended a successful showjumping round with a great leap into the air! He died on July 4th 1999 and is buried on the Whitakers' farm in Yorkshire.

## Desert Orchid

When Dessie ran in his first race in 1983, it seemed like it might be his last. He fell heavily in a hurdle race and took a long time to get back to his feet. But it was his career in steeplechasing that showed his extraordinary willpower and incredible courage, always leading from the front, and never giving up, whatever the conditions and the competition. He won the King George VI Chase four times, as well as other major races such as the Whitbread Gold Cup, the Cheltenham Gold Cup and the Irish Grand National, to name but a few!

Following his retirement in 1991, Dessie made many public appearances, raising thousands of pounds for charity. He returned every year to Kempton Park, the racecourse where he had seen so many victories, to lead the parade of runners for the King George VI Chase. He died in 2006, aged 27.

# horses

It's not just success that makes for an all-time great horse. They have that something special which makes them truly unforgettable. Here are some of our all-time greats. We've only included British horses, but there are loads from overseas, too – and we're sure you'll have your own ones to add!

## Red Rum

**all-time great**

When you think of Red Rum, you can't help but think of the Grand National, because it was this race he won on three occasions, coming second on two others – all between 1973 and 1977.

'Rummie' became one of the best known and most loved racehorses in the UK and Ireland. A national celebrity, he used to go swimming in the sea off Southport before every Grand National race.

A life-size statue of Red Rum stands at Aintree Racecourse, scene of his magnificent victories. Red Rum lived from 1965 to 1995.

## Toytown

**all-time great**

When Zara Phillips first rode Toytown, he was in need of some serious work. His show jumping, in particular, let the pair down to begin with, but he was to go on to some brilliant wins. In 2002, the pair won the Young Rider title at Bramham, followed by individual silver at the Young Riders' European Championships. They then went on to win team and individual gold medals at the European Eventing Championships and World Equestrian Games.

Very sadly, due to injury, Toytown and Zara weren't able to compete at the 2008 Beijing Olympics, having missed the 2004 Athens Olympics for the same sad reason.

## Sefton

**all-time great**

Sefton was a popular (and slightly unusual) member of the Household Cavalry – at the time, the regiment only allowed horses who were black all over, and Sefton had a white blaze and socks! He will be remembered forever for his bravery on the morning of July 20th 1982 when an IRA nail bomb was detonated close to his regiment of horses on their way to the changing of the guards.

Sefton sustained horrific injuries and endured eight hours of surgery, with only a 50:50 chance of survival. But he recovered fully and went back to work with pricked ears. He even walked past the spot where the bomb had gone off without turning a hair! His bravery captured all our hearts and when he retired to The Horse Trust, he enjoyed the attention of countless visitors.

## And the list goes on...!

We'd love to include many more, such as Ellen Whitaker's **Locarno 62**, **Colton Maelstrom** (the prolific winner of pony showjumping classes), **Bonfire** (one of the best Grand Prix dressage horses the world has ever seen), event horses **Be Fair** and **Priceless**, both of whom notched up fabulous wins during the 1970s and 80s, and the brilliant show jumper, **Arko III**, but we just couldn't squeeze them all in!

## Who are your Top 10 all-time great horses?
Compare your choices with your horsey mates!

1................................................
2................................................
3................................................
4................................................
5................................................
6................................................
7................................................
8................................................
9................................................
10................................................

# Duggie's secret stalker!

**Duggie and Soloman were chilling in the paddock**

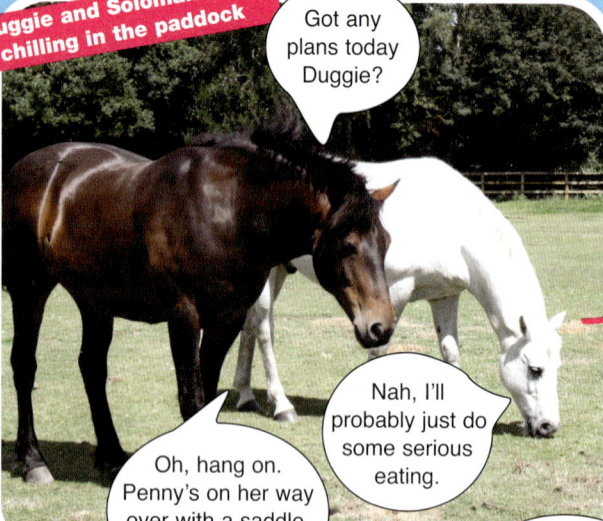

Got any plans today Duggie?

Nah, I'll probably just do some serious eating.

Oh, hang on. Penny's on her way over with a saddle. Will it be me or you?

Hi Duggie, I've come to take you on a lovely hack!

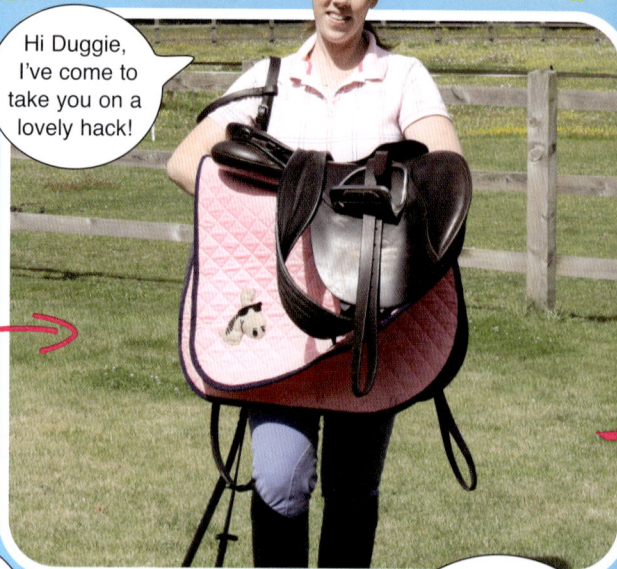

Do you know what Duggie? I've got a funny feeling we're being watched!

Me too! This is freaking me out.

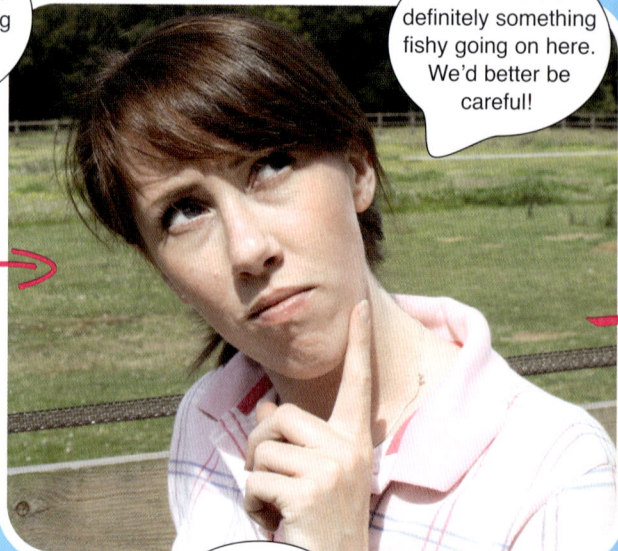

I think there's definitely something fishy going on here. We'd better be careful!

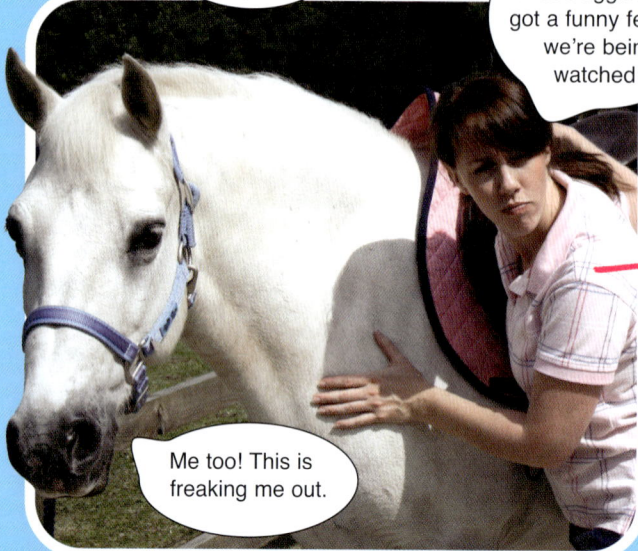

He'd better keep his peepers peeled, I'm sure there is someone dodgy hanging around here.

Ha ha! I'll catch that Duggie out! I'll just go and tell Soloman what I'm going to do.

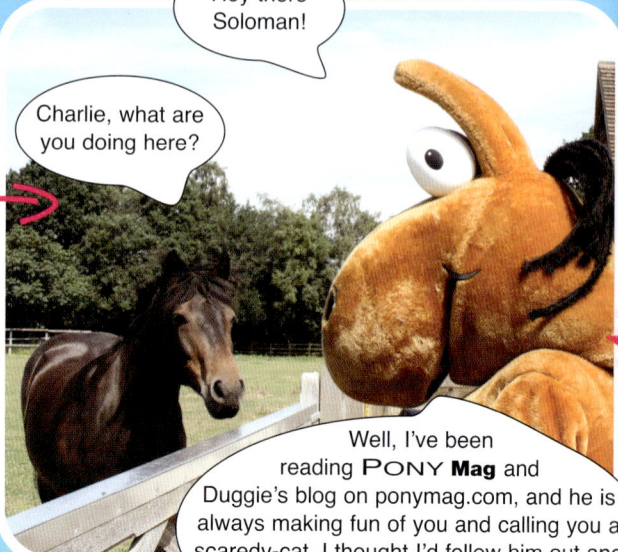

Hey there Soloman!

Charlie, what are you doing here?

Well, I've been reading PONY **Mag** and Duggie's blog on ponymag.com, and he is always making fun of you and calling you a scaredy-cat. I thought I'd follow him out and make him jump – give him a taste of his own medicine!

Charlie

Penny

Soloman

Duggie

There's something fishy going on! Duggie is sure that he's being watched, maybe even stalked by a crazy fan! Who could it be?

**PART ONE**

Looks like it's your turn today, Duggie!

Yeah, yeah. But listen, right. I've got a funny feeling something odd is going on around here. I feel like I'm being watched! I think I might have a stalker!

Of course you have... not!

Come on Duggie, let's get you tacked up.

Okay, but I'm keeping my eyes peeled for crazy, stalking fans!

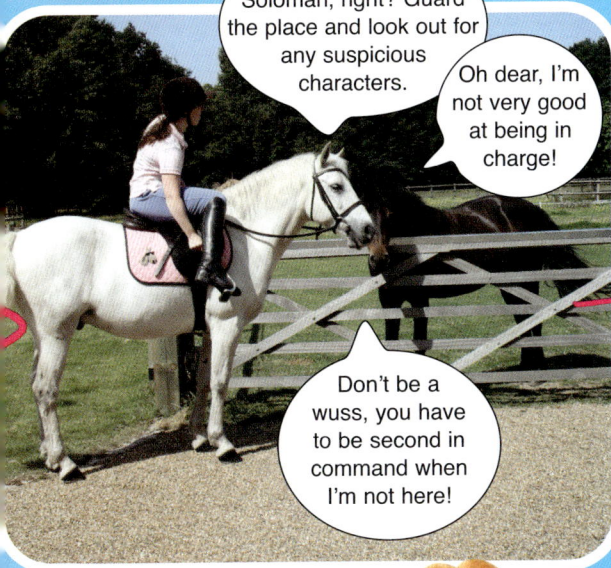

You're in charge Soloman, right? Guard the place and look out for any suspicious characters.

Oh dear, I'm not very good at being in charge!

Don't be a wuss, you have to be second in command when I'm not here!

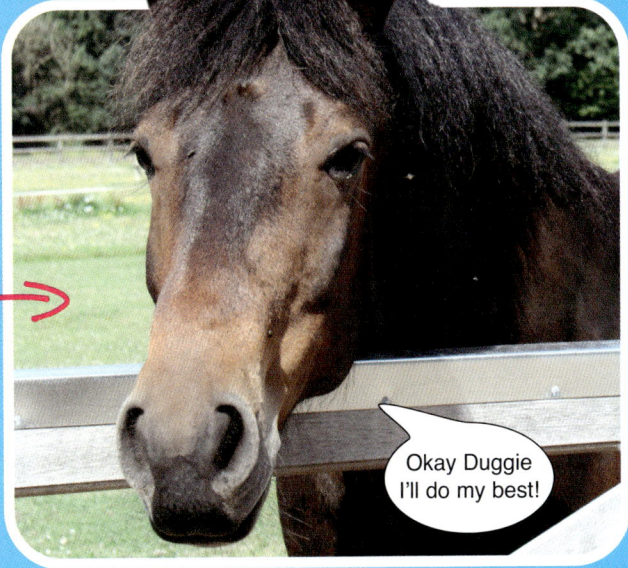

Okay Duggie I'll do my best!

Well leave me out of it, Charlie. You're on your own!

Okay Soloman, I promise I won't tell him that you knew! See ya, I'm off to do some scaring!

Find out what happens next on pages 88 and 89!

▶▶▶ 69

Ever wanted to make a fab Christmas pressie for your mates? Well, PONY tells you how to make your very own pony winter wonderland!

# MAKE A
# PONY
# SNOWSTORM

Fill the jam jar with about two cms of glycerine and top up with water. Add lots of sparkly glitter!

Give the snowstorm mixture a good stir with a paintbrush, so that it all mixes together.

Using strong glue, stick your model pony to the inside of the jam jar lid (feet first or he'll be upside down!). Wait for the glue to dry thoroughly overnight.

**TOP TIP!**
You can check if your jam jar will be leak-proof by filling it up with water and then shaking it around, but make sure you test it over a sink first!

Screw the jam jar lid on tightly, so that none of your special snowstorm mix escapes. You can also put a line of glue inside the lid, so that all leakages are prevented!

Decorate the edge of the lid with a piece of festive ribbon.

Shake the jar and watch your pony in his fabulous glittery winter wonderland!

# What does your stable say about YOU?

Are you tidy or messy, clean or dirty, or maybe a bit in-between? If you don't know, take a peak at your stable. It might reveal loads about your personality!

## GOING IN
Open the stable door, and what's waiting there to greet you? Some dirty, chewed-up and spat-out hay and other unmentionables?

Or, a beautifully swept yard and stable door entrance? Sweeping up may be a pain to do, and it's hard on the arms and back, but, if you keep on top of the dirt and mess, it won't take too long (and you'll tone up those muscles nicely...).

## MUCKY MANGER
If your manger looks like this, just stop to ask yourself how often you eat from plates caked with yesterday's supper. It's not nice, it's not clever, and you should curl up in a corner in total embarrassment.

That's more like it! We're not expecting dishwasher-style cleanliness, but a regular wash and brush to get rid of the worst excesses is a definite must. It's important for your pony's health, and it will make the food taste nicer, too. Nuff said for now!

## COBWEB ALERT!
Stop one moment to look around the stable walls. Are they about to be taken over by an army of spiders because you like to think they kill off the flies, but in all honesty, don't like the idea of sweeping away the cobwebs?

Or do you regularly sweep away cobwebs to keep the stable clean and dust-free? Though spiders are very useful (and cute, some say!), ponies need to be kept in as dust-free an environment as possible, as they can be prone to respiratory problems.

## DRINK UP!
This automatic waterer hasn't been cleaned in ages, which means it's covered in dust on the outside, has soggy leaves, gunk and dribbles of old horse feed on the inside – and doesn't exactly make the thought of drinking from it entirely desirable!

What a difference a clean makes! Considering how important fresh water is for horses' and ponies' bodily systems to work, you should be doing everything you can to ensure that whatever your pony drinks from is squeaky clean.

## BRUSH OFF!

It's not much use if your primary cleaning tool – your broom – is dirty and full of bits of hay and straw (like this one here). You'll end up sweeping old mess into new mess.

## RIGHT MESS!

Mmm...not too sure that ponies will want to eat this hay which has been trodden into the droppings which weren't picked out of the stable. Not particularly appetising, we have to say...

Another really good habit to get into when caring for ponies in stables is to pick out the droppings as often as you can. That stops ponies from standing in their droppings, which are not good for their feet anyway, and it will also prevent hay getting all dirty and messy.

It pays to take the trouble to pull as much of the hay out of it, and give your brush a good wash with a hose from time to time – like the clean one shown here!

So, have you found out whether you are

# NEAT AND TIDY

(like our examples)

## or ULTRA MESSY

(like these)?

If you are the messy type, maybe we need to take a look around your feed room, which may well look a bit like...
THIS! (Oh no, don't go there...)

Be honest now...!

73

# A question of confidence

PONY **Magazine** short story competition finalist!

## By **PONY** reader Tamzin Barnett

I'd thought Conker was perfect. His previous owner had been highly enthusiastic.

"We won our first show – he is so talented and very capable," she'd said. "Conker is the most loving horse anyone could have. He jumps anything and with his paces, he's always placed in the show ring."

"If you like him, Rachel, we'll have him," said Mum.

He is perfect really, it's me that isn't. I sighed and rolled over in the hospital bed. There was a throbbing pain in my arm where I'd fallen off. I wasn't badly hurt, just suffering from shock and a badly bruised arm. My mind wandered back over that day.

"I think the Open is a bit big for you Rachel," Mum had said. "This is your first hunter trial on Conker after all."

"Mum, don't be silly – Conker can do anything! This is easy for him, especially after what we've been doing at home," I'd replied. "And if Jade is entering, I want to as well!" I was sure I was going to win. I'd walked the course really carefully, and although Conker was quite lively, he'd felt

### "Mum, don't be silly – Conker can do anything... this is easy for him!"

fantastic over the practice jumps – but admittedly the jumps had looked huge.

Conker had felt nervous in the collecting ring as we waited to go, jogging excitedly and half-bucking as I held him back. Feeling suddenly nervous myself, I'd tried not to let him know it.

Maybe the Open wasn't such a good idea. Jade had gone before me looking immaculate and calm, Silver cantering with an even stride towards the first fence. They'd met it perfectly and disappeared up the track. I was called in next and the steward counted us down. Conker did a mini rear and by now I was feeling really scared. The whistle blew – he leapt forward like a rocket, taking me by surprise, his mane flying in my face. I'd tried to relax, but the first fence looked

quite solid and I was terrified! Conker rushed towards the fence in a wild, strong gallop. I could never jump it like this! He met it all wrong, legs in a tangle – crash! I fell from his back, sinking through the darkness. I had one last thought – I'll never ride Conker again.

Weeks later, the sun shining for the last week of the Easter break, it was Jade who was schooling Conker in our field, glaring at me in frustration.

### "He met it all wrong, legs in a tangle – crash! I fell from his back, sinking through the darkness."

"You could at least try," she said glowering. "I have my own horse to ride as well. We should be riding together!"

"Jade, I can't, you know that. You're doing me such a favour, and you know you love riding him." But I looked at Silver in the field. He was putting on weight. Since Jade had been riding Conker she said she hadn't had enough time for both ponies.

"Why don't *you* ride Silver?" Jade insisted for the hundredth time.

"I told you, I don't want to ride." I still felt a rush of panic at the thought. I stroked Conker's velvet muzzle. His summer coat was beginning to show a beautiful rich, red-brown against his black points and white socks.

Jade sighed and turned him away, breaking into trot, which became a canter, toward the jump we had set up. Conker gathered speed, but Jade held him back and gave him a sharp smack on the shoulder with her whip which made him lurch sideways. He cat-jumped the fence and tried to gallop off. Jade pulled him onto a tiny circle until he was stationary again. Although I hated seeing him ridden like this, I wished I had Jade's confidence.

When I walked into class on the first day of term, I overheard Jade talking to some our friends.

"Oh, Rachel doesn't ride at all now," she smirked, "she's too scared. She just

gives her horse treats and mucks him out. I'm the one who actually rides him. Her mum doesn't know anything and I expect they'll have to sell him."

I was too embarrassed to reply.

"She had a bit of a fall in the hunter trial and won't get on her pony again," Jade continued.

"My mum says you should always get back on after a fall. I always do," one of our friends said. "Falling off proves you're a real rider, anyway."

"Yes," agreed Jade, "there's nothing scary about falling off. Not that I remember anyway, I haven't fallen off for ages."

I suddenly felt angry and shouted "Shut up! I couldn't help falling off! You've never had a fall like that, Jade! I bet if you'd had a new horse and had a fall like that, *I'd* be riding it for *you*!" I rushed out and Jade and I ignored each other for the rest of the day.

I hated Jade now. What was I going to do? I couldn't ask her to ride Conker again and I couldn't ride him. I knew what my mum would say. And she said it that evening when I brought Conker in.

"I think you should ride him again, Rachel. He seems to be settled with Jade. We're paying all this money and he's wasted, someone else could be using him. If you're really set on not riding him, we should think very seriously... so you either ride him or –"

"Or?" I challenged, already knowing the answer.

"Or he goes," Mum replied.

"No!" I cried. Over by Silver's stable, Jade seemed to be having an argument with her mum, too. I glanced at her and she glared back. Then Jade's mum started walking over to us, Jade following gloomily – her arms crossed, in tears!

"I'm afraid I've got news that concerns all of us." She looked around at each of us. "We're moving to Norway for three months – Tony's been stationed there." Jade's dad was in the army.

"I know it's a lot to ask but would you be able to take Silver on while we're away? He's quieter than Conker," she added with a glance at me.

"Silver might really boost Rachel's confidence," my mum said. "I'm sure we'll manage."

I looked at Jade, who rolled her eyes at me in silence. We both knew Silver was lovely to ride and completely reliable – so why was I beginning to shake? I took a deep breath.

"I'll try to ride Silver," I said.

Later, when we got home, Mum brought up the inevitable subject again.

"Maybe you could ride Conker again when Jade's gone. I know Conker and Silver are inseparable now, and he's such a lovely horse. It would be such a shame to let him go. But..."

I panicked.

tears. We flicked through the pages, which showed Mum, younger than me, and a beautiful roan pony.

"That was when I first got her. Sherbet Fountain." My mum smiled. "And this was at our first show, and this –"

**"I couldn't believe it. No-one had ever mentioned that Mum had ridden, ever."**

I couldn't believe it. No-one had ever mentioned that Mum had ridden, ever. Or jumped the very large cross country fences I could see in the photos.

"Then one day," said Mum, "we entered a one-day-event. The dressage was difficult and the jumps were bigger than I'd ever done before. We were lying in second before the cross country. Half-

again after that."

"And you never told me," I whispered.

"No. But now we're going to pull ourselves together. We've got a great horse there, and he deserves us, too."

"Rachel, outside rein, inside leg." Silver immediately responded as I followed my mum's instructions. She was riding Conker on a circle in a perfect outline.

"Are you ready to jump?"

"Are you?" I called back.

"Turn into the jump from trot. Half-halt if he wants to canter. I'll follow on." Silver sailed over the fence perfectly and suddenly my confidence soared. I turned to see Conker and my mum float over the fence without breaking their relaxed rhythm. It was three months since Jade had left, and Mum and I had hacked and schooled, each of us remembering the fun we'd once had.

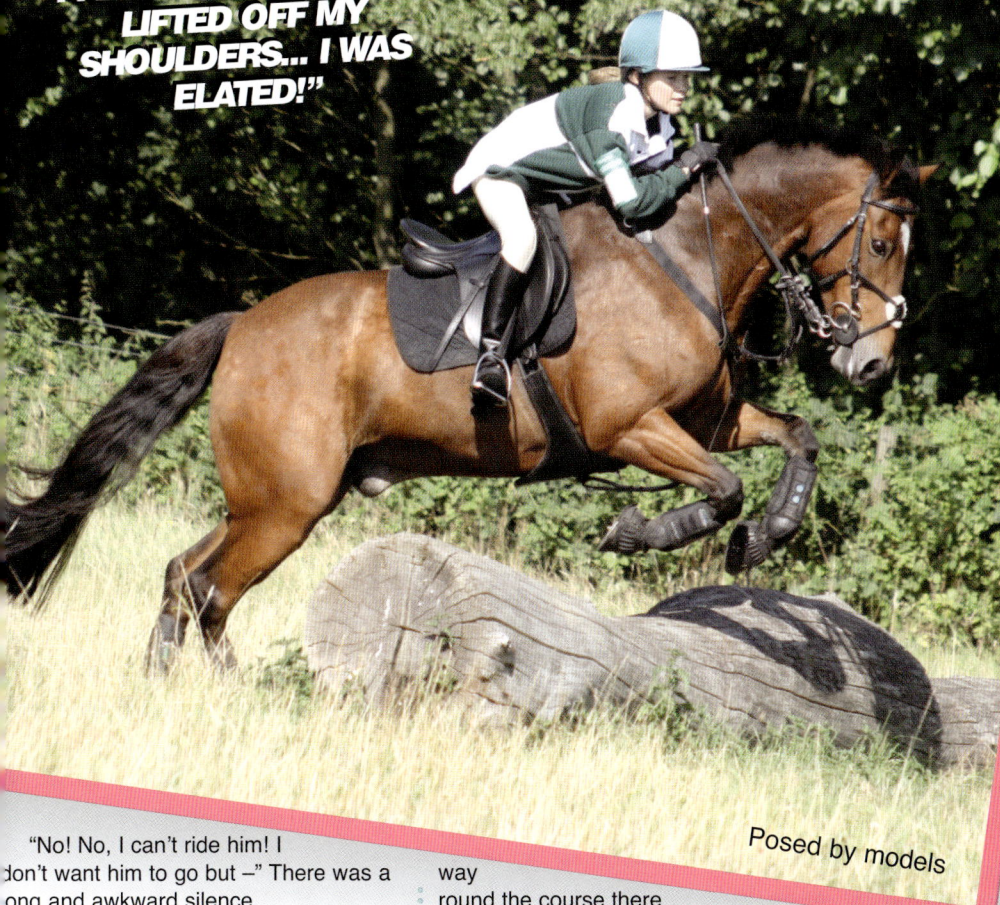

*"I FELT A HEAVY WEIGHT LIFTED OFF MY SHOULDERS... I WAS ELATED!"*

Posed by models

"Rachel," Mum called, sliding off Conker. I knew what she was going to say, and I rode over in excitement. I had butterflies in my stomach as we swapped horses. Conker seemed huge! I led him to the mounting block, pushing my fears away. As I swung into the saddle he looked round at me, his ears flickering, and as he moved off, his powerful walk felt wonderful. I asked him to trot and he responded without rushing. By the time we'd finished, I'd cantered and jumped and I felt a heavy weight lifted off my shoulders. Mum was grinning at me and I felt so elated.

"Rachel, Rachel!" A familiar voice called from the yard. It was Jade! She rushed up to us.

"No! No, I can't ride him! I don't want him to go but –" There was a long and awkward silence.

"Well," said Mum slowly. "There is someone who could ride him."

"Who?"

"Me."

"Don't be stupid Mum! You've never sat on a horse in your life!" My mum went to the cupboard, slowly brought down an old case, and placed it on the table. It was quite tatty and I'd never taken any notice of it before. When she took the lid off I gasped – it was full of rosettes! Mostly red. Mum rummaged through to the bottom and brought out an old photo album. I could see she was in

way round the course there was a big spread. Sherbet took off too soon. She never made it. There was a sickening crack when we hit the fence. I just remember lying on the other side of the splintered wood, the two of us. There was a lot of blood. I cried and cried... and I never really understood why they could mend my leg and not hers. I never rode

**"We're going to pull ourselves together. We've got a great horse there, and he deserves us, too."**

"I just saw you jumping Conker! Well done you! To be honest, I never thought you'd have the nerve! Silver looks fantastic, who's that riding him so well?" My mum was at the far end of the field, leg yielding towards us.

It took some explaining, and everyone at the hunter trials that autumn was surprised to see my mum in the open class. And although I was really nervous, I knew she'd be okay.

And she won.

# PUZZLE FUN!

## Super Sudoku

Each line must have one of each pony's head in it. Try to figure out where each one should go!

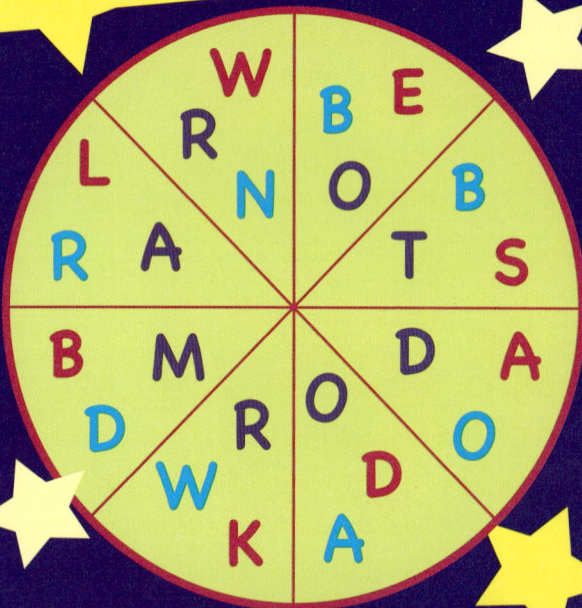

## Wheel of fortune

Using one letter from each traingle, spell the name of a breed, a pony colour and the name of a piece of tack. Each letter can only be used once! (They are colour-coded to help!)

## Trophy maze

Help the horse to find his way to the trophy so that he wins the competition! Make sure you follow the lines carefully!

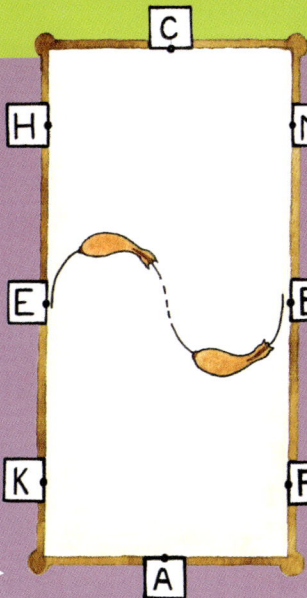

Use the letters from a normal dressage arena to work out the answers. The X markers show you which letters to use!

## Wacky wordsearch

Try to find all these words in the wordsearch — be really careful as they might be upside down, or going diagonally!

| Caspian | Ergot | Filly |
|---------|---------|---------|
| Annual | Coronet | Mare |
| | Azoturia | |
| Pony | Colt | Stallion |

| | | | | | | | |
|---|---|---|---|---|---|---|---|
| r | e | p | o | k | n | e | n | g | q |
| w | a | o | n | x | r | n | p | f | n |
| a | n | n | u | a | l | c | t | i | a |
| n | a | y | m | n | n | e | o | l | z |
| h | i | b | n | a | n | g | l | l | o |
| o | p | n | k | o | v | n | r | y | t |
| n | s | n | r | n | y | n | e | n | u |
| s | a | o | n | h | j | d | a | n | r |
| e | c | o | t | b | s | v | i | n | i |
| c | s | t | a | l | l | i | o | n | a |

## Scrambled words

Unscramble the letters to make five famous riders name.

1 APIPP LNEFLUN

2 LENEL KWRITEHA

3 NBE HMARE

4 RAZA LIPSHIPI

5 MWILAIL HAKEWTIR

## amazing answers

The answers can be found on pages 96-97! Why not challenge your friends?

## Blurred vision

These photos of everyday yard items have been blurred. Can you still tell what they are?

## Book-tastic!
Long distance rides by N. Durance

77

# You know you'r

...you prefer the smell of fresh hay to pizza!

...you have to get your horsey fix every week or your life is over!

...all your schoolwork includes something about a pony, no matter what subject you are learning about!

...you wash your hair with horsey shampoo!

...all your birthday presents are horsey, with no make-up in sight!

...your fave pony's stable is tidier than your bedroom.

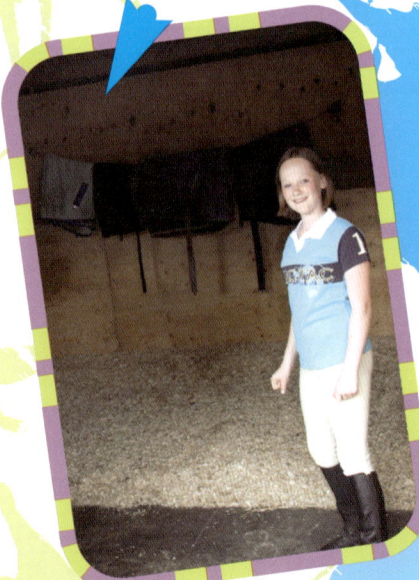

...you get detention for filling in a competition entry form during English!

...you own more pairs of jodhpurs than you do jeans!

...your pocket money goes on Polo's rather than sweets for you!

...you have every horsey film ever made, and you can repeat them word-for-word as you watch them all the time!

# ADDICTED to ponies when...

...your fave pony's neigh is your ringtone on your mobile!

...you sometimes write your pony's name rather than yours on your schoolwork, and your school books are smothered with your fave pony's name, rather than pop or movie stars!

...you rush to the window whenever you hear hooves going past your house!

...you talk about your fave pony in your sleep!

...the riding school starts asking for rent because you spend so much time with your fave pony!

...you pretend your muesli is coarse mix!

...you can't see the colour of your bedroom walls because they are totally covered with pony posters!

...you put up jumps at weekends and jump over them just like a pony – sound effects and all!

...you practise your dressage test on foot while your pony eats his lunch!

# Confident Caspians

## Terrific temperament
The Caspian horse is renowned for its kind temperament. It is intelligent, willing to please and very genuine. Even the stallions can often be handled and ridden by children.

## Fab fact!
Although Caspians are only small, they are always classed as horses because of their head and body shape, regardless of their size. When photographed without a handler next to them, they often look as if they are much bigger — more like an Arabian or a Thoroughbred size.

## Cracking conformation
The Caspian's conformation has improved massively since the breed was first discovered, due to a mixture of selective breeding, quality feedstuffs and higher standards management. Another benefit is that the Caspian can often work barefoot, as the feet are small and incredibly strong.

## Semi-feral
Small numbers of Caspian horses still exist in a semi-feral state in the rice paddies, cotton fields and forests of the remote Elburz mountains in North Iran, near the Caspian Sea.

## Perfect horse

The Caspian horse makes a wonderful mount for a child, capable of competing in all disciplines. It is pretty enough for the show ring, and is a natural jumper, with lovely paces.

Caspian sea

## Fab fact!

Caspian horses have an extra molar tooth in their top jaw, as well as a different shaped head to other horses and ponies. This proves their ancestral links with Egyptian paintings of ponies pulling the Royal Chariots of the Persian King, Darius the Great, as these had the same head shape.

## Ancient connections

The Caspian was only recently re-discovered in 1965, having been originally found by the Greeks 2,500 years ago. They are one of the world's most fascinating ancient horse breeds and represent a link between the early breeds of Equus and today's 'desert' horses.

## Scurry horses

Nowadays, the Caspian is often used for scurry driving. Due to their sloping shoulders and long, free action, the Caspian is fast enough to keep up with larger horses at every pace except for the gallop.

## MINI QUIZ

Read through the following statements and decide if they are true or false. Write your answer in the space provided and then check the answers to see if you were right!

**1** Caspian horses can gallop faster than larger horses.

True ☐ False ☐

**2** There are still some semi-feral Caspian horses in the wild.

True ☐ False ☐

**3** Caspian horses have an extra molar tooth in their top jaw.

True ☐ False ☐

**4** The Caspian is never used for driving as it is too slow.

True ☐ False ☐

**5** The Caspian horse is one of the oldest breeds in existence today.

True ☐ False ☐

5. True.
4. False, the Caspian is often used for scurry driving.
3. True
2. True
every pace except the gallop.
keep up with larger horses at
1. False, Caspian horses can
**ANSWERS**

# THE NAME'S BOND... CHARLIE BOND!

Hey Mum, guess what? My friend Susie is having a big party for her birthday!

Wow, that sounds fun. What is she doing?

Well, it says on the invite that it's Hollywood theme, so I guess we have to dress up as film stars!

Hello, what are you gossiping about?

Look Charlie, my friend Susie is having a Hollywood party!

Excellent!

Now, what shall I wear...? Who are you going as Charl?

Now whoa there mister, Whoever said anything about you coming?!

But you've got two tickets! All your friends will already be invited, and it's not like you have a boyfriend to take...!

Shut up Charlie!

Well you haven't!

Now stop it both of you!

Charlene, you have two tickets so take you brother with you, and Charlie... please stop winding your sister up!

Hurry up Charlie, we are going to be late!

Oooh, Marilyn Monroe eh?

And who *exactly* are you supposed to be?

I'm James Bond of course! Look, I even got this cool watch from a fancy dress shop that talks back to me if I ask it a question!

Whatever! Let's get going.

Charlie, if you're hanging around with me can you try not to embarrass me please.

SUSIE'S HOLLYWOOD PARTY

Oh, don't you worry, I'm off to find some fillies to chat with!

Why does my brother always have to show off?

And of course, being James Bond, I have all the cool gadgets like this spy watch

Aagghhh!

Some James Bond... I think you'll find that's a clown's watch Charlie!

# My friend is jealous of me

**Jenna and Daisy had been best friends for ages, going to school and having riding lessons together. But all that changed when stable heart-throb Lewis asked Daisy out on a date...**

## THE BEST OF FRIENDS

My best friend, Jenna, and I are both 15, and we've known each other since we were five and were in the same class at primary school – that's when our interest in horses and ponies started. Jenna's mum was a keen horsewoman, so it was inevitable that Jenna was going to follow in her footsteps. She started having lessons at the local riding school and when Mum and Dad heard how much fun she was having, they agreed to me having lessons as well.

## WHAT A HEART-THROB!

We had a great time and as we got older, we were allowed to go hacking and spend part of the summer holidays on *Own a Pony* weeks. In fact, this became an annual treat for us both and we really looked forward to it.

Most of our riding friends were girls – and some came from the same school as us. However, there was a boy called Lewis, who kept his pony at the riding school, and he was gorgeous. He was two years older than us and had a weekend job at the stables, mucking out and grooming. He had dark hair and huge blue eyes, and he was always very friendly to me. All the girls thought he was cute, so I was flattered that he was so attentive to me. It made going to the stables even better!

## OUT OF CHARACTER

Lewis and I seemed to have lots in common and enjoyed each other's wacky sense of humour. At weekends, we'd sometimes eat our lunch together and catch up on the week's news. But I was always aware of Jenna staring at us. We asked her to join us one day, but she just turned her back on us and stomped off. This was totally out of character for Jenna, because she was always so friendly to everyone – and then I discovered the reason for her strange behaviour...

**Lewis was always very friendly to me – I was flattered he was so attentive**

## MAKING A DATE

One of my other riding friends, Sam, told me that Jenna had admitted to having a crush on Lewis. She'd fancied him for ages apparently, and had decided she was going to pluck up the courage to ask him out! However, when Lewis asked me if I wanted to ride his pony, Jester, and then asked me out on a date, Jenna went a bit strange, and it wasn't like her, at all.

She started getting nasty and would hardly talk to me at school, let alone when we were at the stables together. She said I'd changed, that I didn't talk to her any more and that I ignored her when Lewis was around. However, that couldn't have been further from the truth! I always tried to include her in the things we were doing, but she wasn't having any of it – she would just ignore me.

## SPREADING THE WORD

And now, because Lewis and I are officially going out together, that's made things even worse. He always lets me ride Jester, whereas Jenna still rides the riding school ponies. Lewis had actually offered her a ride on Jester, but she just snubbed him and said some hateful things to me – such as when Lewis dumps me, I'll have no friends left – and that sticks in my mind. And even our other riding friends won't have anything to do with me any more because Jenna has turned them against me, which makes me really sad.

Riding is my hobby and I'm supposed to enjoy it, but at the moment, I don't and it's tearing me apart. I understand why Jenna feels the way she does, but there's nothing I can do about it. Lewis really likes Jenna and wants her as a friend, just as I do. But I'm not going to let the situation with her get me down and hope that we can be friends again. I won't ignore her or be horrible about her, the way she has done with me, and only hope that she realises she's throwing away our years of friendship.

A real friend would understand – I'm just sorry it had to end this way.

**I only hope Jenna realises that she's throwing away years of friendship**

posed by models

83

# Make
# A pony stained-glass window!

## Help to give your bedroom a warm glow by making a fabulous stained glass window!

## You'll need
- Scissors
- White pencil
- Glue stick
- Coloured tissue paper
- Dark-coloured card

### Step one

Use our templates on pages 98-99 to make a Christmassy-pony picture. Draw around each template with a white pencil onto dark card.

### Step two

Cut out the shapes carefully.

### Step three

Glue pieces of tissue paper to the back of the card. Try to use lots of different colours to make the picture glow more!

# Step four

Turn the card back over and admire your picture, then stick it in the window, and watch the light shine through your Christmas stained glass window!

**Hang them up and enjoy the warm glow!**

HAPPY CHRISTMAS!

# 10 ways your

## 1 Be a copycat

● Watching good riders is inspirational and will give you lots of ideas of how you can improve your own riding. If you see a pony going well, copy what the rider is doing!

● Watching bad riders shows you what to avoid doing! If you see a pony going badly, try to see what the rider might be doing to cause it. Then avoid doing the same thing!

## 2 Develop feel

Good riders feel what their pony is doing underneath them. Can you tell which leg is leading as you canter? Do you know whether your pony is standing square when you halt? Take a look, then absorb how that feels and remember it. Test yourself until you get it spot on!

## 3 Could it be you?

If you think your pony's doing it all wrong, ask yourself what *you're* doing to cause it. Sort *yourself* out, and you could find suddenly that your pony miraculously improves!

# upgrade riding!

**T**ry these guaranteed ways to turn your riding around and give yourself an upgrade!

## 4 Look up, look where you're headed!

Keeping your head over your shoulders has an instant, positive affect on riders. You don't see Ellen Whitaker or Carl Hester looking at the ground, do you? They look up and ahead of them. What better recommendation can you have?

## 5 Be a snooty rider!

No, we're not talking hankies, we're talking attitude. When you're riding, imagine you're a snooty, looking-down-her-nose at everyone sort of rider. It will make you sit tall and elegant in the saddle. Slouching is banned!

## 6 Use a mirror – it's in a good cause

Is there a mirror in your school? It's not there so you can check your hair! Use it to be critical about your riding. Are you straight or wonky? Are you lopsided? Is one hand higher than the other – or your shoulders unlevel? How about your stirrups? Is one longer than the other? That's what mirrors are for!

## 7 Change your attitude

Do you moan when you're given the riding school slowcoach? Are you cross when the pony you ride tanks off with you? Negative vibes mean you won't learn anything from the ponies you ride. Turn it around! These ponies are a challenge and will teach you loads – so why not *ask* for a tricky pony next time?

## 8 Make your hands a pair

Give your hands some attention. As you ride, is your left higher than your right? Does one go haywire while the other one stays still? Does one turn inward, the other out? Lay a whip across both your hands, tucking your thumbs over it and ride like that for a while. Your hands will have to work as a pair and you'll find your pony goes along like a dream – what a difference!

## 9 Work with a partner and both improve

Ride with your best mate and give one another positive feedback. You might be able to tell her that her legs are too far forward, which is why she's finding it difficult to balance at rising trot. She could let you know that your head's all wonky, and making your pony go round in circles. Remember not to criticise – you're supposed to be helping one another, not falling out!

## 10 Keep an open mind that's what it's for!

The very best riders know they never stop learning. Every pony will teach you something new – providing you want to learn. Treat your riding as a wonderful exploration of discovery and you'll soon be a much better rider!

# Duggie's secret stalker!

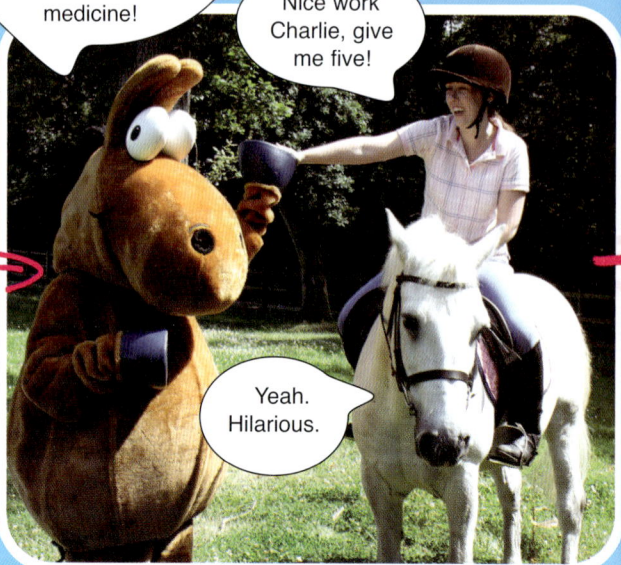

Will Duggie spot Charlie before he gets the chance to make him jump? Read on and find out!

Charlie

Penny

Soloman

Duggie

**PART TWO**

Snigger!

Come on Duggie, there's no-one there.

I'm not so sure about that!

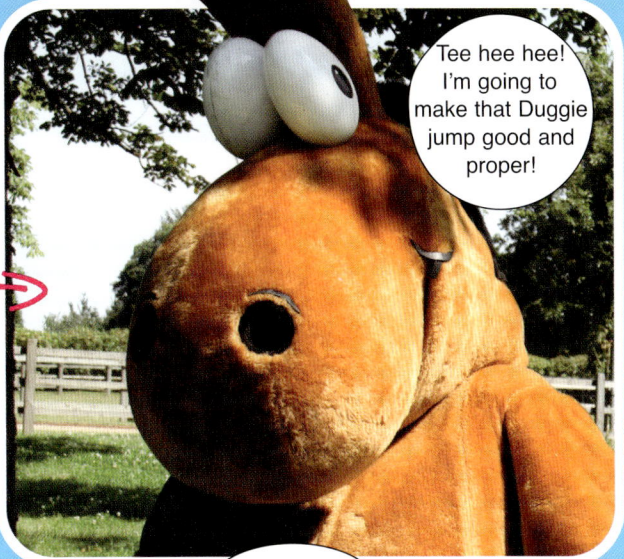

Tee hee hee! I'm going to make that Duggie jump good and proper!

Here he comes, I just hope Penny doesn't fall off!

Booooooo!

Aaggghhhhh!

Charlie! Whatever are you doing here?

Oh pur-*lease* Soloman, you knew Charlie was following me!

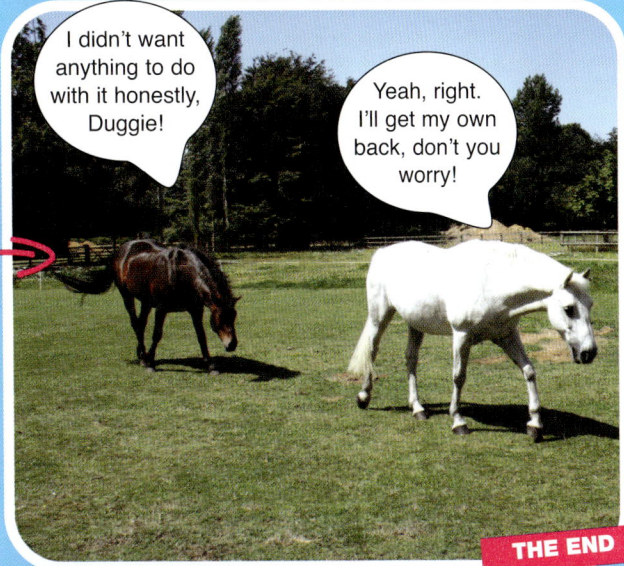

I didn't want anything to do with it honestly, Duggie!

Yeah, right. I'll get my own back, don't you worry!

**THE END**

## DECEMBER

Thoroughbred racehorse broodmares are turned out by day from August until January. With their winter coats, good food and sheltered paddocks, they live comfortably together in small, friendly groups.

## JANUARY

The foaling season starts in January and a watchful eye is kept on all expectant mothers. It's a very exciting time for everyone at the National Stud!

**DYK?**
Pregnancy in mares takes about 11 months.

## FEBRUARY

The National Stud staff will know when it is almost time for the foal to be born. Mares who are due to foal in the next few days go over to the special Foaling Unit with huge foaling stables. The Unit is manned 24 hours a day so there is always someone there to help the mare when she goes into labour.

**DYK?**
January 1st is the official birthday of Thoroughbred horses!

# BROOD MARE

The National Stud at Newmarket has 500 acres of fabulous grazing and stables for highly valuable Thoroughbred stallions and mares. The stallions and mares may be big race winners, worth millions of pounds! We went to see what life is like for a Thoroughbred brood mare and her future champion foal!

## MARCH

Once her foal is born, the mare and foal go to the Nursery Yard. At first, the mare and foal are turned out alone for a few hours, so that the foal can get confident and steady on its feet.

When the foal is approximately four weeks old and the mare comes into season, she may visit the stallion to be put in foal again.

**DYK?**
The foals at the National Stud are taught to lead from a very young age, walking beside their mothers. A stud hand leads the mare from the offside, the foal from the nearside, so that the foal gets used to being led from this side.

**DYK?**
A foal is up on its feet within an hour of birth, and suckling almost immediately.

**DYK?**
Foaling takes around 20 minutes!

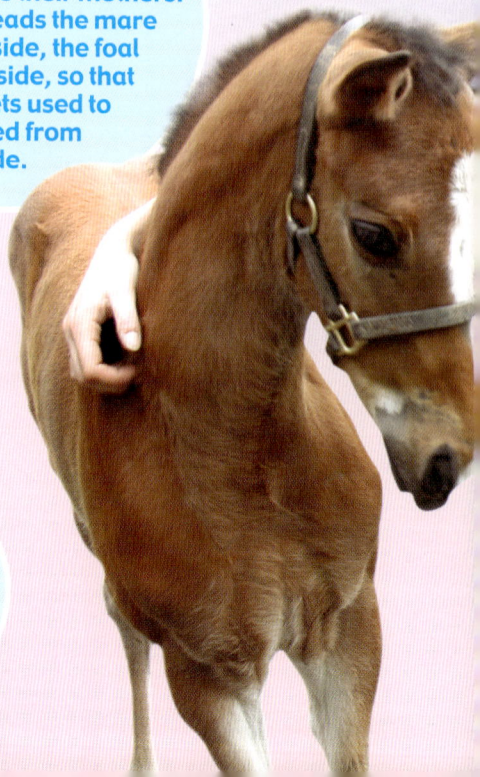

# DIARY!

**1 Jan**

## APRIL

Small groups of three mares with foals the same age are turned out together. The mares have company and the foals have each other to play with!

## MAY

The mares and foals will now be turned out day and night to enjoy the summer.

## JULY

Six months after birth, the foals big enough to leave their mothers are gradually weaned. The youngsters don't mind too much as they have their friends to keep them company.

The mare is then turned out again until late December/early January, and the cycle starts all over again!

## WHAT ABOUT THE FOALS?

National Stud weanlings may go to the bloodstock sales and be snapped up by an owner as a racing prospect. Who knows, they may be future Derby winners! Sometimes the weanlings are kept at the stud until the following year, when they go to the sales as yearlings.

The weanlings and yearlings can fetch many thousands of guineas. If they have a famous racing sire and dam, they may even make *millions* of guineas!

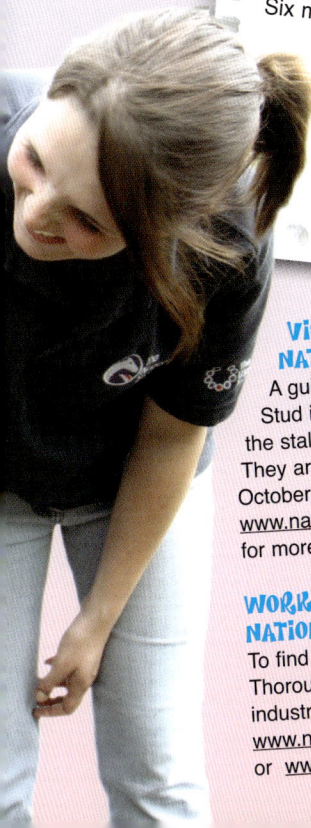

## VISIT THE NATIONAL STUD!

A guided tour of the National Stud is a fabulous way to see the stallions, mare and foals! They are held from March to October. Go to www.nationalstud.co.uk for more info!

## WORK AT THE NATIONAL STUD!

To find out about careers in the Thoroughbred racing or breeding industry go to www.nationalstud.co.uk/education> or www.careersinracing.com.

91

16 pairs of muscles in the ears enable them to move independantly in all directions!

The forelock is for protection against flies, dust and muck, as well as sunlight. It is also pretty nifty for filtering water down and away from the face and eyes when it rains.

Muzzle — the most sensitive area of the body with many feelers, whiskers and especially soft skin.

Horses are not colour blind. They can see blues and green quite distinctly but it may be difficult for them to see red and to distinguish yellows from green and blue.

Eyes set wide on the head give great all-round vision, but horses do have two blind spots directly under their noses front and directly behind them.

Adult horses have between 36 and 44 teeth used for eating, grooming and fighting!

Horses' membranes — the gums, inside the nostrils and around the eyes — are a great indication of equine health. They should be a nice pinky colour, neither pale nor yellow or pink and inflamed.

A highly acute sense of smell is used for interpreting messages given out by predators, other ponies, plants (or food) and the surroundings.

At rest, an average of 12 breaths per minute are taken.

There are no muscles below the knees and hocks to keep the legs light so horses can run fast.

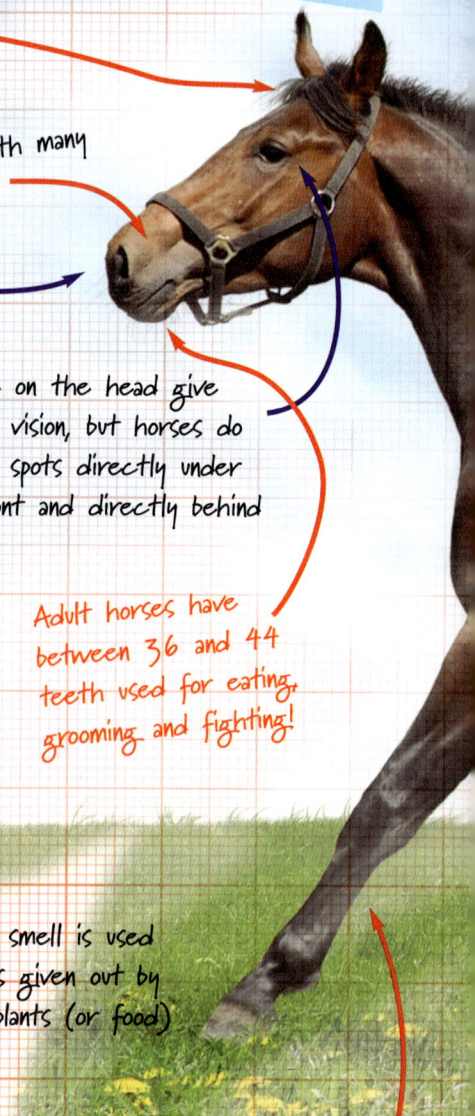

60% of the bodyweight is carried on the front legs.

Have you ever thought about how horses and ponies are put together? We think they are perfectly designed, do you?

...sting heart rate of ...adult horse or ...ny should be ...tween 36 and 42 ...eats per minute. Can ...o up to around 240 ...eats per minute ...during hard exercise!

The coat is naturally water repellent. The oily substance that coats the hair comes from sebum glands below the surface of the skin.

Normal body temperature – 38 °C (100.5 °F)

All horses have whorls. These are points on the coat where the hair changes direction. Found on the head and neck, they are good for identification.

The skeleton has approximately 205 bones giving the body structure.

The tail – an excellent fly swatting device and also allows water to run down and off the body when it rains.

The hooves grow around 10cm per year. Good feet should slope at an angle of around 45 to 50 degrees.

The hair on the stifle grows upwards to direct rain away from the tummy area as the hair here is fine. The hair on donkeys' stifles does not grow up like this because they are from hot desert countries where it doesn't rain very much.

Horses possess the ability to lock their stifle, enabling them to relax their muscles without falling over so they can sleep standing up!

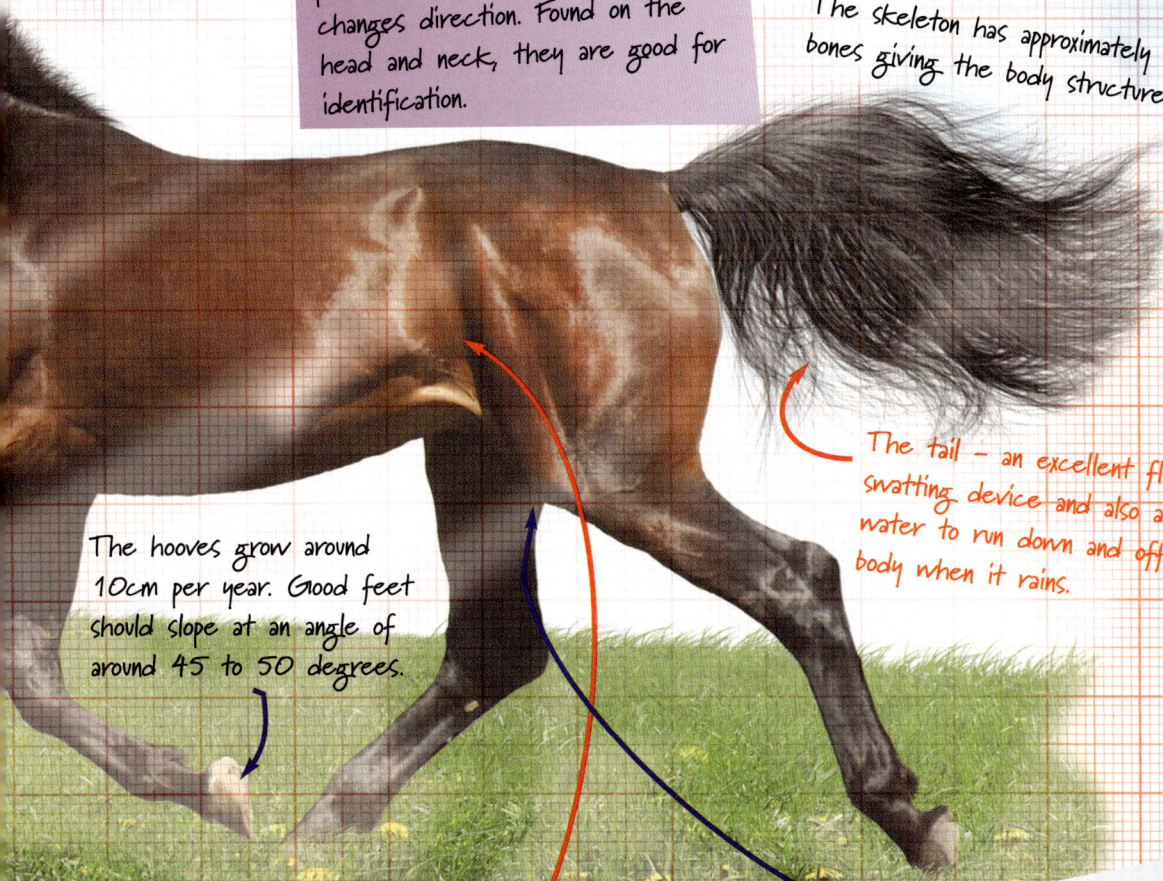

*Jorja and Molly mistime their hack and get caught in the dark, and then their ride starts to go horribly wrong...*

## Thursday

I don't know about you, but I think there is something so very cosy about tucking your pony up in bed at night and just watching them pull at a haynet. I utterly adore doing that with Jigsaw, especially when it is cold and frosty. I was doing exactly that the other night; I was leaning over her half door, telling Jigsaw how much I loved her, when suddenly someone dug me in the ribs. I shot about a metre in the air – I mean, wouldn't you? It was Matt, of course!

"Gotcha!" he cried, laughing.

"That is *so* not funny Matt!" I told him. My heart was beating like a drum.

"Did you think I was a ghost?" grinned Matt?

"Ha ha, very funny. Of course not!"

"Yep, you did!" Matt went into CP's stable and left me with my pounding heart. That woke me up!

## Friday

Devon was particularly tiresome today. She tied Raven up outside her stable and Star immediately leant out and nipped the black mare's neck. Devon wasn't amused.

"Can't you control that ill-mannered pony of yours, Molly?" she asked in her usual, supercilious manner.

"Oh give him a break," exclaimed Molly, "Raven's in his face!'

"I'm not being funny, Molly, but it's obvious where he gets it from," remarked Devon. Which was a bit harsh, I thought.

Molly just glared at her. Devon refused to move Raven so Star kept on harrassing her, causing Raven to pull back and break her rope.

"I believe you owe me a rope, Molly," Devon said.

Molly pulled a face. "Yeah, good luck with that!" she cried. "What is it with that girl?" Molly asked me when Devon had saddled up and gone in the school.

"Not getting on with the lovely Devon?" asked Matt, annoyingly.

"Don't you start..." Molly warned.

"What?"

Molly threw a dandy brush at Matt.

## Saturday

Molly and I both went for a great hack this afternoon. The trouble was, we set off a bit late and the light started to fade when we were still miles and miles from home.

"Connie will be sending out a search party for us," said Molly.

"I'll ring Matt so he can let her know we're on our way," I offered, hitting the speed dial button. Matt answered – eventually.

"Where are you?" he said when I'd explained the situation.

"Miles away. We're at Owl's Hill and we'll be at least another 40 minutes, even if we hurry."

"Okay, I'll tell Connie!" Matt said, "but do you know those woods are haunted?"

"Oh don't say that!" I cried.

"Don't look behind you!" laughed Matt, and rang off.

"What's he saying?" enquired Molly, looking round.

"He says these woods are haunted!" I told her.

"Rubbish!'

We set off for home. The ponies were a bit spooky in the fading light, and we trotted around the fields towards the woods.

"Star just wants to gallop," said Molly, tugging on the reins.

"Star *always* wants to gallop," I pointed out. By the time we got to the woods, the darkness was closing in. It was dead creepy. Woods always seem sort of cosy and friendly in the daylight, their branches wrapping around you in a big woody cuddle. In the gloom of twilight, they seemed downright hostile, their branches drew us in and threatened never to give us up again. The wind was picking up and all around us was a clattering and rustling sound.

"You don't suppose..." Molly began, "... that Matt was right, do you?"

"Shut up, I'm freaked out enough already," I told her, stroking Jigsaw for courage.

"There's talk of *the hand* that chases riders through the trees," Molly continued.

"Shut UP!" I hissed. The thought of a dismembered hand chasing us like something out of the Addam's Family wasn't cheering in the least.

Suddenly, Star shied violently, spun round and crashed into Jigsaw. Jiggy put her ears back and snapped at him as he rushed past, and Molly's leg crashed into mine.

"Ouch! Get a grip, Star!" I shouted, forgetting to whisper. But Star was beyond getting a grip, galloping back along the path we'd just came along. Out of habit, I made Jiggy stand still instead of following Star, but when Star and Molly disappeared completely I wished I hadn't.

Jiggy and I were alone. In the gloom. And I didn't know what to do. Should I follow Molly or wait for her to come back? But before I could make up my mind I heard an eerie sound ahead. A sort of *wailing*.

I felt all hot. Would a dismembered hand wail? I couldn't imagine how. Jiggy stood stock still, her ears pointing straight ahead, her head up. She didn't seem scared.

I was.

I didn't know what to do. Stay? Go? Follow Molly? Suddenly, Jigsaw whinnied and I jumped a mile.

"Oh, don't do that!" I scolded her, cuffing her mane in fear. And then something even worse happened;

"*I can seeeeee you!*" wailed a very spooky voice.

That was it! Turning Jiggy round, I thumped her in the ribs with my legs and set off after Molly for all we were worth. We caught up with her coming towards us.

"It's okay, I'm all in one piece!" grumbled Molly.

"Run for your life – there's something after us!" I screamed.

"What?"

"I don't know, just turn around and go – now!"

"Not until I know what it is," Molly said bravely – and a bit annoyingly. Jiggy slithered to a halt, pleased to be with Star again. As we stopped, I could hear that, that *thing* coming along the path towards us.

"It sounds like a horse," said Molly. I couldn't believe she was being so

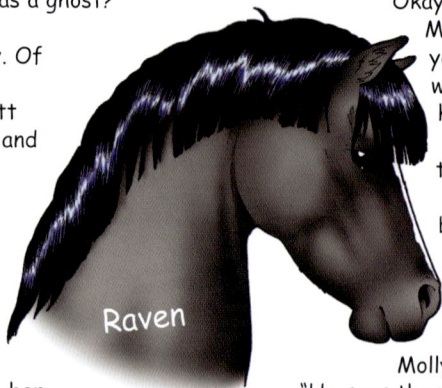

Raven

# ~~HOSTS!~~

*Catch up with Jorja and her pony-mad friends every month in* PONY **Magazine**.

alm and sensible. But she hadn't heard ↑ wailing. But then when I listened, it *did* sound like a horse.

*"I'm coming to get you!"* wailed the ↓oice. A voice that sounded familiar.

"Come on, follow me!" said Molly, ↓teering Star off the track and behind ↓ bush. Jiggy got behind him just in ↓ime for us to see a chestnut pony ↓hunder through the undergrowth past ↓ur hiding place.

"Matt!" we both exclaimed.

"How dare he!" I said. I couldn't ↓elieve Matt was so devious, scaring ↓ne like that. And I couldn't believe I'd ↓allen for it!

"Come on, we'll give him a taste of ↓is own medicine," promised Molly, ↓rging Star onto the path and following ↓P. It was almost dark now, and we ↓ould hardly see a thing, but the ↓onies didn't seem bothered.

"Ye ha, we're coming to get you ↓Matt!" screamed Molly, making me ↓ump again. We caught up with CP by ↓he pond. The ponies were all pleased ↓o see one another and Matt grinned ↓t us. At least, I think that's what he ↓id, I could just make out his teeth in ↓he darkness.

"Got you good, Jorja!" he said.

"Yeah, well, I knew it was you!" I

lied, my heart thudding.

"You're an idiot, Matt, now we're even further away from home," Molly pointed out.

"We'd better get going, then," said Matt and we set off again. "You do know these woods really are haunted, though, don't you?" he said.

"Yeah, yeah, give it up for goodness sake," groaned Molly.

"I can't believe you still believe in ghosts, Matt," I said, trying to keep my beating heart under control.

Suddenly something floated across the path right in front of us. Something white and silent. Without speaking, we all urged the ponies into canter to get out of the woods as quickly as possible. Luckily, the moon came out from behind a cloud, bathing the woods in moonlight and lighting the way ahead.

We didn't stop cantering until we were almost home.

"I hope Connie doesn't see the ponies in this state," puffed Molly. Jiggy and CP were sweating and Star was all fired up, throwing his head around and jogging.

"What *was* that?" I said, shivering.

"A ghost. Had to be!" whispered Matt. I looked across at him and he

winked. Molly said nothing.

With Star all rugged up and settled, Molly went home – her dad had been waiting in his car. My mum wasn't due for another half-an-hour so Matt and I sat in the barn and shared a Kit-Kat.

"That was *so* scary!" I said, shuddering as I remembered the white shape floating past us all.

"I wasn't scared," bragged Matt, cramming two Kit-Kat fingers in his mouth at once.

"Come off it, you were so. And it so serves you right for trying to scare us both before!"

"That wasn't a ghost – don't you know what that was?"

"Okay Mr Clever-cloggs, what was it then? Come on!"

"An owl. They never make a noise when they fly. There aren't any ghosts in the woods."

"Oh Matt, you could have said so at the time! I suppose you're right, there are no ghosts in the woods," I said, with relief. I felt a bit silly.

"That's right," said Matt, picking mud off his jodhpurs. "All the ghosts live at the farm!"

Matt just managed to jump off the hay bale and run before I could hit him. He is *soooo* annoying!

# We have the answers!

Want to find out how you did on the puzzle pages?
Well, here are the answers!

## Answers for Puzzles pages 28 – 29

### Wordsearch

```
f p s y r i t s k s r e a n s e
h c h e s t n u t e a h s m e r
i k v r i m l b n e s i o y a v
e r n g a c r e m e l l o j t n
l p o f w r r s t t l m l n q m
w o i m e l f u o i c n a d b h
i i d e b i k s p e p o p s l w
z i d w b a c k d x s t p p i e
c s l c r a a i h s g e a t d i
f c e w o t l r s z y l d x l u
s a l e w l b d a c o a c b a y
g i t d n e m a r m g n a s b t
c v g u b s u p i a l d n m w r
r o a n t l n o n p t t a e s
e p r p r b o o n e a t l m k r
a c t j l a c g y e n f e y s t
```

### Crazy questions!
1) **Brushing is when the hoof or inside of the fetlock strikes the inside of the opposite leg.**
2) A dorsal stripe is a dark stripe running along the spine from wither to tail.
3) **Knee boots are used when travelling or riding on the roads.**
4) Linseed is good for putting on condition and giving a glossy coat.
5) **Ragwort is a common wild flower with yellow petals that is poisonous to horses and ponies.**
6) Studs are used to give horses better grip, especially when jumping.

### Picture crossword

```
¹B R U S ²H
A      ³E Y E S
A       A
Y      ⁴D R I V I N ⁵G
        C       I
        O       R
⁶B R I D L E     T
I       A       H
T      ⁷R U G
```

### Spot the difference

## Wheel of fortune

The breed found in the wheel is the *Dartmoor*.
**The pony colour found in the wheel is *skewbald*.**
The piece of tack found in the wheel is a *browband*.

## Blurred vision

1) Plastic tubs
2) Shavings fork
3) Manure scoop
4) Wheelbarrow
5) Body brush

## Super sudoku

## Blurred vision

## Trophy maze

The first line lets the pony reach the trophy.

## Scrambled words

1) Pippa Funnell
2) Ellen Whitaker
3) Ben Maher
4) Zara Phillips
5) William Whitaker

## Wordsearch

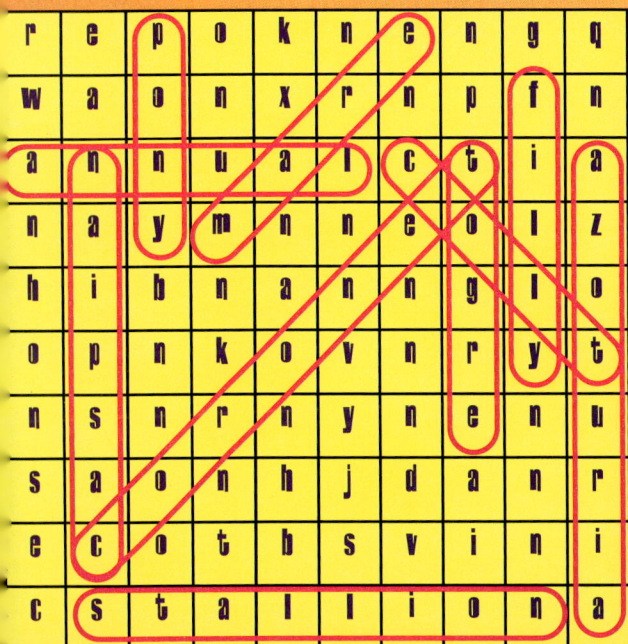

## Puzzle arena

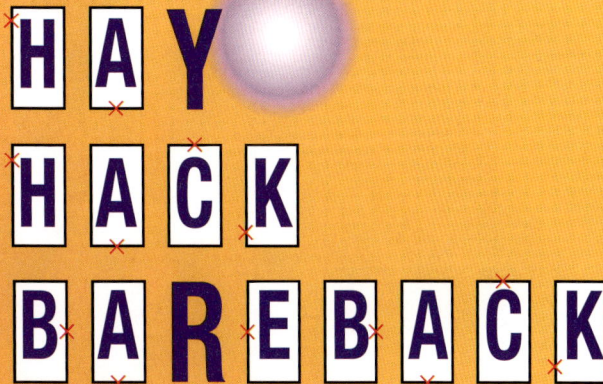

# THE LAST LAUGH!

You're nearly at the end of your Annual, time for a few laughs, courtesy of the PONY team. Why not have a joke contest with your mates and see who can make you laugh the most?

**TEE HEE!**

Why did the pony have to gargle? **Because it was a little hoarse!**

**What is a horse's favourite TV programme?** Neigh-bours!

**GIGGLE!**

What do you say to a sad horse? **Why the long face?**

**CACKLE**

**Carly: My pony is a real gentleman.** Natalie: Why? **Carly: Because whenever we come to a jump he stops and lets me go first!**

**A man rode his horse to town on Friday. The next day he rode back on Friday. How is this possible?** The horse's name was Friday.

**CHORTLE**

What do you g[ive] a pony with a co[ld?] **Cough stirrup!**

When does a horse talk? **Whinney wants to!**

**CHUCKLE**

**What did the horse say when it fell over?** I've fallen and I can't giddyup!

**GIGGLE!**

Here are all the templates, cut outs and counters you need for all the funky makes, and also for the Duggie board game! Cut around the dotted lines carefully and have fun!

# Templates, cut outs and counters!

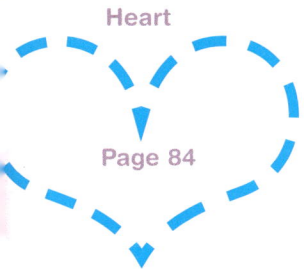

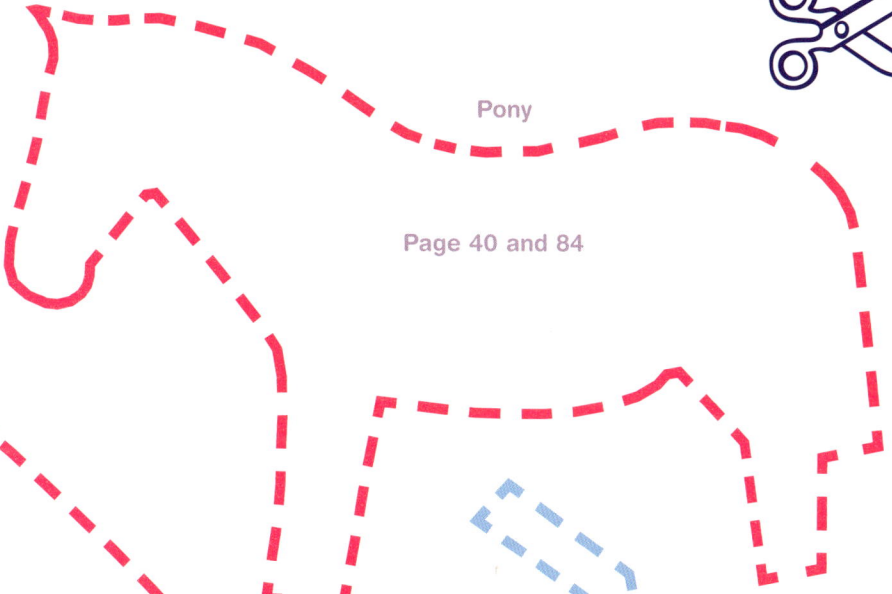

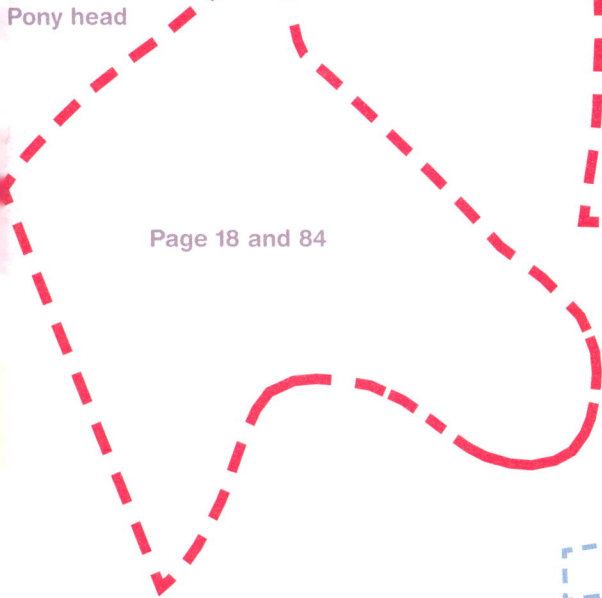

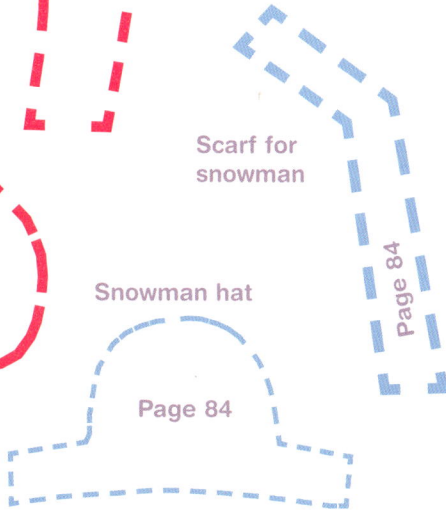

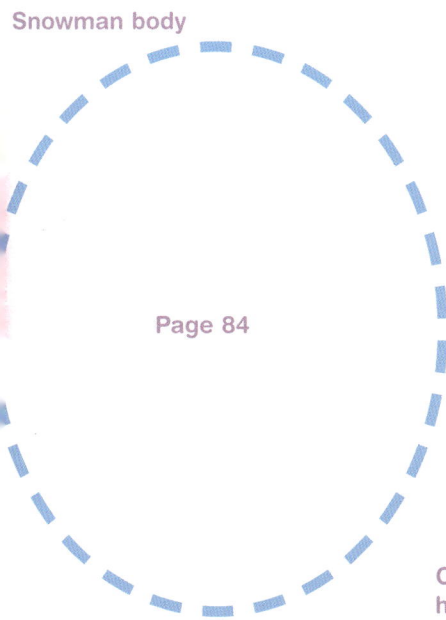

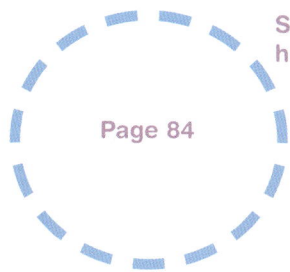

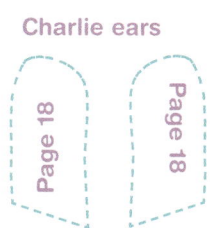

Heart

Page 84

Pony

Page 40 and 84

Pony head

Page 18 and 84

Scarf for snowman

Page 84

Charlie

Snowman hat

Page 84

Snowman body

Snowman head

Page 84

Soloman

Charlie ears

Page 84

Page 18

Page 18

Duggie

Page 84

Charlie head

Page 18

Page 18

Charlie glasses

Colonel

99

www

It's
the next
best thing
to riding!

www